THE SECRET POWER OF JOY

MARK HANKINS

THE SECRET POWER OF JOY

MARK HANKINS

Scripture quotations marked TLB are taken from The Living Bible: Paraphrased by Kenneth Taylor. Copyright © 1971 by Tyndale House Publishers.

Scripture quotations marked 20th C.R. are taken from The Twentieth Century New Testament, Revised Edition Copyright 1900, 1901, 1902, 1903, 1904 by Fleming H. Revell Company.

The Secret Power of Joy Second Edition 2017
ISBN#978-1-88-9981-39-0

Published by
Mark Hankins Ministries Publications
P.O. Box 12863
Alexandria, LA 71315
www.markhankins.org

Printed in the United States of America

Table of Contents

Consider it MAXIMUM JOY, my brothers, when you get involved in all sorts of trials…well aware that the testing of your faith brings out steadfastness. But let steadfastness have full play, so that you may be completed and rounded out with no defects whatever.

- James 1:2 - 3 (Berkeley)

1

Count It All Joy

My brethren, count it all joy when you fall into various

trials, knowing that the testing of your faith produces

patience. But let patience have its perfect work, that

you may be perfect and complete, lacking nothing.

- James 1:2 - 4 (NKJV)

I used to eat microwave popcorn just about every night and got pretty good at making it! It took exactly three minutes and 45 seconds in our microwave. If I was going to watch a football game, I would put a bag in the microwave, set the time and get my soda ready. Then I would come back to check the progress of the popcorn. I'd look through the window (that's why they put them there), and nothing would seem to be happening. One minute, then two and a half minutes would go by, and nothing changed. The bag was still lying motionless in the microwave. Just when I was about to give up, I'd hear, "Pop!" Then, I'd hear another, "Pop, Pop!" For the next minute, that sound would fill the kitchen until the entire bag was popped!

It is the same principle with the things you are believing to receive from God. You have God's promises from the Word, but at times it seems like nothing is changing— nothing is happening! Just as I had to do with that bag of popcorn, you've got to keep on waiting. You've got to keep your joy level set on high and expect to receive. James 1:2 says you've got to count it all joy. I like what James 1:3 says in *The Berkeley Translation*, "...well aware that the testing of your faith brings out steadfastness. But let steadfastness have full play, so that you may be completed and rounded out with no defects whatever."

Joy gives you patience or staying power. It helps you to stay in a position of faith while God is working a miracle in your life—while He's working all things together for your good (Rom. 8:28)! If you rejoice while you wait for the answers to your prayers, it won't be long until you hear "pop!"

TURN IT UP TO TEN JOY!

Consider it maximum joy, my brothers, when you
get involved in all sorts of trials….
- James 1:2 (Berkeley)

He did not say that it was a "joy" to have multiple troubles. He said to "count it joy." Look at your problems and count. One joy…two joy…three joy…then laugh at the devil! What Satan meant for evil, God is turning around for your good. Jesus paid too high a price for your victory for you to be defeated. Ha! Ha! Ha!

One time I put my bag of popcorn in the microwave, set the timer, and walked away to do something else. When I returned, the bag had not popped. How disappointing! I checked the time and then I checked the bag. Finally, I looked at the settings on the microwave and I found the problem! Someone had set the microwave on defrost! I said, "Trina, did you set the microwave on defrost?" She replied, "Yes dear." So I turned it back on high, set the time again, and soon I heard that "pop" that I expected.

Maybe you have not been getting any answers to prayer and victory seems lost. Maybe it's been awhile since you've heard a "pop" in your life. Check your joy level. You may need to get your rejoicing off defrost and set it on high!

I like to say it this way: when you're going through difficult times, turn your joy up! Remember, we're supposed to count it ALL joy—in both the good times and the troubled times. The word "all" in the Greek is *pas* and includes all the forms of declension.[1] That just means that the word joy in this verse encompasses every level of joy—from cheerfulness and calm delight to gladness and exceeding great joy.

As you begin to count your situation "all joy," then, you may start at "1-joy" which would be to brighten up. Then comes a smile which gets you to "2-joy," a chuckle at "3-joy," and so on, all the way to "10-joy"! This "10-joy" is the same joy Peter referenced when he told us to rejoice with "joy unspeakable and full of glory" (1 Peter 1:8). *The Amplified Bible* calls it "TRIUMPHANT, heavenly joy!" This kind of joy has winning power in it!

Your joy may be simmering right now, but you can turn it up to maximum "10-joy" and get the full manifestation of whatever you're believing for! You may say, "I don't really have anything to rejoice about." Let's see what Habakkuk has to say about that.

> *Although the fig tree shall not blossom, neither shall fruit be in the vines; the labour of the olive shall fail, and the fields shall yield no meat; the flock*

shall be cut off from the fold, and there shall be no
herd in the stalls: YET I WILL REJOICE IN
THE LORD, I WILL JOY in the God of my
salvation.

- Habakkuk 3:17 - 18

Here is a clear picture of how to "count it all joy" when every circumstance around you is negative. The Hebrew word for "rejoice" here is *alaz* and means to jump for joy—to exult, be joyful, rejoice, and triumph.[2] Think about it. Even children naturally jump up and down when they're happy.

But can you jump for joy? How can you rejoice in terrible times? You can rejoice because you know something besides what is obvious to your physical senses. James 1:13 says, "Let no man say when he is tempted, I am tempted of God: for God cannot be tempted with evil, neither tempteth he any man." Remember God is not the one who is tempting or testing you. That is not His nature, but every good and perfect gift comes down from Him (James 1:17). God has given us the power through His Word to stay in a position of faith. 2 Peter 1:3 says, "According as his divine power hath given unto us all things that pertain unto life and godliness, through the knowledge of him that hath called us to glory and virtue." Jesus said in John 16:33 that, "...In the world ye shall have tribulation: but be of good cheer; I have overcome the world." There is a crown of life given to those who overcome the tests and afflictions from the devil (Rev. 2:10).

I BROUGHT YOU HERE TO HAVE A GOOD TIME

Several years ago, Trina and I took our children to Disney World in Florida. It is such a creative and exciting place for children with a lot of rides and entertainment. It is also quite an expensive trip for any family. I thought it was funny when I saw a mother scolding and correcting her little boy for whining and complaining. The mother grabbed him firmly by the arm and said, "I brought you here to have a good time, and you're going to have a good time!" The mother commanded him to stop complaining and whining, and to get happy right away. She went on to explain to the boy why he was commanded to have fun. She said, "I paid too much for this trip for you to be grouchy and complaining. It has taken us too long to get here for you to ruin it with your whining!" The little boy promptly dried up his tears, stopped whining, and enjoyed the rest of the trip. I laughed because I understood exactly how that mother felt.

ENJOYING THE TRIP

Now I can imagine our Father God having a similar problem with some of his children. I can hear Him saying:

> *I brought you here to have a good time – now you are going to have a good time! I paid too much for your freedom for you to be bound – I paid too much for your joy for you to be depressed – I paid too much for your peace for you to be confused – I paid too much for your forgiveness for you to be condemned – I paid too much for your righteousness for you to be guilty or ashamed – I paid too much for your healing for you to stay sick – I paid too much for your success for you to fail!*

The price of our freedom was the precious blood of Jesus. Jesus paid too high a price for our blessing for us to be cursed. We are blessed in Christ. God is speaking to us saying, "I brought you here to have fun – NOW YOU ARE GOING TO HAVE FUN!" Jesus even prayed for us to experience His joy and gladness as He prayed in the Garden before His crucifixion. John 17:13 says, "And now I am coming to You; I say these things while I am still in the world, so that My joy may be made full and complete and perfect in them [that they may experience My delight fulfilled in them, that My enjoyment may be perfected in their own souls, that they may have My gladness within them, filling their hearts]" (AMP). It is time to enjoy our victory in Christ! It is time to enjoy our redemption!

REJOICE – YOUR NAME IS WRITTEN IN HEAVEN

The Lord is a God of salvation, help, deliverance, healing, and provision—and you know Him! That's what Jesus taught His disciples. In Luke 10:20, He said, "Nevertheless do not rejoice in this, that the spirits are subject to you, but rather rejoice because your names are written in Heaven" (NKJV).

No matter what bad things happen in life, at least you're not going to hell! That's something to be happy about! Jesus was certainly happy about it. Verse 21 says that, "in that hour Jesus rejoiced in the Spirit" (NKJV). *The Spirit Filled Life Bible* has a note on this verse, commenting on how Jesus rejoiced. "The successful mission of the 70 caused Jesus to burst forth in a spontaneous demonstration of worship in the Spirit (the Greek word suggests shouting and leaping with joy)." [3]

You can rejoice about the fact that you are saved regardless of your circumstances. Even if your best friend just left you, you can say, "ha, ha, ha! At least I'm not going to hell!" Rejoice, shout, and leap for joy because your name is written down in Heaven! Rejoice, because with God, nothing is impossible. Rejoice while you are waiting for the answers to your prayers, and you'll soon hear "pop, pop!" You have just hit "10-joy"!

1 James Strong, *The New Strong's Exhaustive Concordance of the Bible* (Nashville: Thomas Nelson Publishers, 1984) G3956.

2 James Strong, *The New Strong's Exhaustive Concordance of the Bible* (Nashville: Thomas Nelson Publishers, 1984) H5937.

3 Hayford, J. (2002). In J. Hayford, *The Spirit Filled Life Bible* (p. 17). Nashville, TN: Thomas Nelson Publishers.

Serve the Lord with gladness….

- Psalm 100:2

…Bring a gift of laughter.

- Psalm 100:2 (MSG)

2

Laughter – The Best Medicine

A merry heart doeth good like a medicine: but a broken spirit drieth the bones.

- Proverbs 17:22

A glad heart makes a healthy body....
- Bible in Basic English

A glad heart is excellent medicine, a spirit depressed wastes the bones away.

- The Jerusalem Bible

I once read a newspaper article titled, "Stress Relief Found in Laughter Clubs," that I found quite interesting. It talked about how laughter clubs are being formed across the nation and around the world. Basically, people gather to laugh. They even have a World Laughter Tour and train laughter leaders. The article described today's world as full of busy, stressed out people. World problems, personal problems, money problems, and family problems, along with constant negative news of violence, death, and destruction, have made people frustrated, worried, and unhappy. The world is finding out what God's people have practiced for thousands of years! You've got to attack every situation with a laugh—even if you have to force one out to start.

HA, HA, HA—I'M ON MEDICATION

A merry heart really does good like a medicine and a broken spirit does make one sick. Just naturally speaking, laughter, happy emotions, and expressions of joy release endorphins that relieve pain. I like to say that some people's endorphins haven't been out for so long, that if they did come out, they would be dressed seventies' style! Even psychologists say laughter is the best way to deal with stress and its mental and physical effects. Laughter improves our health, helping our immune system fight disease, lowering our blood pressure, and fighting heart disease. The best thing about it is that it is one of the medicines prescribed by our Heavenly Father, the Great Physician. Let's take a closer look at the physical benefits of laughter.

According to Dr. Gjerdingen, a family physician and professor at the University of Minnesota Medical School, humor promotes good health.

> *Humor is defined as a stimulus that helps people laugh and feel happy, while laughter is a response to humor that involves positive physiological and psychological reactions. The positive emotions associated with laughter and humor involves the dopamine system of the brain. When one laughs, various muscle groups are activated, but the period after the laugh is characterized by general muscle relaxation, which can last up to 45 minutes. Greater relaxation is seen with true laughter, compared to simulated laughter.* [1]

Melissa Breyer, an author for "Healthy Living," shows what happens physiologically and psychologically when a person laughs. Here are just a few things it does:

- *Lowers blood pressure*
- *Increases vascular blood flow and oxygenation of the blood*
- *Gives a workout to the diaphragm and abdominal, respiratory, facial, leg, and back muscles*
- *Reduces certain stress hormones such as cortisol and adrenaline*
- *Increases the response of tumor and disease-killing cells such as Gamma-interferon and T-cells*
- *Defends against respiratory infections (even reducing the frequency of colds) by immunoglobulin in saliva.*
- *Increases memory and learning in a study at Johns Hopkins University Medical School, humor during instruction led to increased test scores*
- *Improves alertness, creativity, and memory.* [2]

"Humor and creativity work in similar ways," says humor guru William Fry, M.D., of Stanford University. "By creating relationships between two disconnected items, you engage the whole." [2]

Have you ever seen the television commercial advertising a drug to help you sleep that has a butterfly floating through the window and around a peaceful, sleeping lady? I was watching it and thought, "Hmmm, I'd like that. I've never had a butterfly come in my window while I'm sleeping. Maybe I should get some of that." Then they begin to read all the possible side effects of this particular medication. "This medicine may cause rapid heartbeat, stroke, nervousness and sleeplessness, dry mouth, nausea, blood clots, and thoughts of suicide and depression. It may cause you to never enjoy romance again." Whoa! Change the channel! Butterflies or no butterflies, I don't want that medication. Get it far away from me!

You've got a better choice prescribed by Dr. Jesus, the One Who made you. His laughter medication doesn't have any negative side effects! All you'll experience is the joy of the Lord. Who knows, you may even get addicted to laughing at impossibilities! That's okay. Smith Wigglesworth said, "Faith laughs at impossibilities."[3] You may be having an impossible challenge now, but stop whatever you are doing and laugh right now. If people think you are strange when you are laughing and rejoicing, just tell them, "I'm on medication." Cast your worries and anxieties over on the Lord and His joy and peace will flood your heart, mind and emotions. Learn to laugh at every situation. Learn to laugh even at yourself. Learn to laugh with God, the Creator of laughter. Come on, join God's laughter club, and attack all of life's problems with a laugh.

THE LANGUAGE RECOGNIZED
AROUND THE WORLD

I've traveled in many nations, seen different cultures, and heard all kinds of languages, but when I hear someone laugh, I can always tell they are happy. Like love, joy is a language shared by the world. I suppose as children of God—made in His image—we all have the capacity for laughter. Joy, however, is a fruit of the spirit and originates from a different place—not from your mind or circumstances, but from your innermost being, or your "belly," as Jesus said in John 7:38.

One minister friend of mine was having some serious symptoms in his body and went to see a well known doctor about them. After being examined, the doctor's prescription for my friend was 10 "belly laughs" a day. He thought it was odd, but his physical problem was caused by stress and that deep belly laugh brought him the benefits he needed.

Heavenly, triumphant joy springs out of truth that you know in your heart. It's the truth that if God be for you, then who can be against you (Rom. 8:31)—the truth that if you are in Christ, then old things are passed away and everything is new (2 Cor. 5:17)! Even in times when it seems you have lost everything and you're flat on your back, you can look up to Jesus and let that laughter bubble up out of your heart. You can rejoice in the Lord and take His strength, which is His joy! Ha, ha, ha!

GOD'S JOY — YOUR STRENGTH

In Lester Sumrall's book, <u>*Pioneers of Faith*</u>, he gives this account of one of his personal visits with Smith Wigglesworth. "One day, I asked him, 'Bro. Wigglesworth how is it that you look the same every time I come? How do you feel?' He bellowed at me like a bull and said, 'I don't ever ask Smith Wigglesworth how he feels!' I asked, 'How do you get up in the morning?'"

"He said, 'I jump out of bed! I dance before the Lord for at least ten to twelve minutes—high speed dancing. I jump up and down and run around my room, telling God how great He is, and how glad I am to be associated with Him and to be His child.'" [4]

After this Wigglesworth would take a cold shower, read the Bible for an hour, and then open his mail to see what God would have him to do that day. He was an extremely remarkable man, totally sold out to God.

Psalm 16:11 says that in God's presence is fullness of joy. Brother Wigglesworth learned how to tap into God's strength by rejoicing before the Lord, and drawing on the joy found in His Presence. You can do the same. According to Nehemiah 8:10, "...the joy of the Lord is your strength." *The Amplified Bible* says it this way: "...and be not grieved and depressed, for the joy of the Lord is your strength and stronghold."

This supernatural joy and strength will give you staying power when everything around you falls apart.

REJOICING RELEASES RESURRECTION POWER

It was a Sunday morning after the service had ended, when a doctor in our church approached me with a very serious expression on his face. He had brought a nicely dressed gentleman whom he explained was a minister from another state. This minister had come for surgery, which was scheduled for the next day, and wanted prayer. In the natural, the report was very negative, but the power of the Lord was present as I exhorted him to believe God. Then I laid hands on him, cursing the cancer and releasing the anointing to heal him in Jesus' Name. He fell to the floor under the power of God, and Trina and I danced, laughed, and rejoiced, taking off in a victory run! We looked foolish, but the doctor started to praise God with us as he saw the power of God at work.

The next day, this man went into surgery. When they cut into the area where the cancerous tumor had been, they began to call other doctors to examine this minister. It was agreed that the tumor looked as if it had already undergone radiation and was dead! They plucked it completely out and sewed the man back up. He recovered and was completely free from the disease!

Laughter releases resurrection power that melts down disease. Laugh at disease, laugh at torment, laugh at lack. 1 John 3:8 (AMP) says, "...the reason the Son of God was made manifest (visible) was to undo (destroy, loosen, and dissolve) the works the devil [has done]." The Son of God was manifested to destroy the works of the devil, and the language of laughter will loosen and cause a meltdown of all the power of hell! Ha, ha, ha!

Remember, the Spirit of God who raised Jesus from the dead lives in you. Romans 8:11 says just as God raised Christ Jesus from the dead, he will give life to your mortal bodies by this same Spirit living within you.

Resurrection power resides in every believer because of the Holy Spirit's indwelling power! It is released by faith. Faith is believing and speaking and the language of faith can sound like laughter. Laughter that comes from your spirit and is targeted at an impossible situation, will direct a flow of resurrection power that will give life to your body. It can turn impossible situations into a testimony of God's grace!

Whatever your situation is today, do as Job did, and laugh at destruction and famine (Job 5:22). Open your mouth and speak to your mountain. Let your endorphins loose and release your faith in God with a laugh! Not only will it release your endorphins but it will release your faith.

1 Dr.Dwenda Gjerdingen, M. M. (2012). *The Network A Called Community of Women.* Retrieved January 2012, from http://ag.org/wim/index.cfm.

2 Breyer, M. (2011, August 23). *Care2 Make a Difference.* Retrieved January 2012, from Care2: www.care2.com/greenliving/8-health-benefits-of-laughter.html.

3 Wigglesworth, S. (2001). *Ever Increasing Faith.* New Kensington, PA: Whitaker House.

4 Sumrall, L. (1995). *Pioneers of Faith.* Maple City, MI: Sumrall Publishing.

Whom having not seen, ye love; in whom, though

now ye see him not, yet believing, ye rejoice with joy

unspeakable and full of glory: receiving the end of

your faith, even the salvation of your souls.

- 1 PETER 1:8 - 9

3

Joy: The Bridge Between Believing and Receiving

Faith has a beginning and faith has an end; it has a goal. The Apostle Peter talked about this in 1 Peter 1.

Wherein ye greatly rejoice, though now for a season, if need be, ye are in heaviness through manifold temptations: That the trial of your faith, being much more precious than of gold that perisheth, though it be tried with fire, might be found unto praise and honour and glory at the appearing of Jesus Christ: Whom having not seen, ye love; in whom, though now ye see him not, yet believing, ye rejoice with joy unspeakable and full of glory:

Receiving the end of your faith, even the salvation of your souls.

- 1 Peter 1:6 - 9

Pure gold put in the fire comes out of it proved pure; genuine faith put through this suffering comes out proved genuine. When Jesus wraps this all up, it's your faith, not your gold, that God will have on display as evidence of his victory. You never saw him, yet you love him. You still don't see him, yet you trust him—with laughter and singing. Because you kept on believing, you'll get what you're looking forward to: total salvation.

- 1 Peter 1:7 - 9 (MSG)

Without having seen Him, you love Him; though you do not [even] now see Him, you believe in Him and exult and thrill with inexpressible and glorious (triumphant, heavenly) joy. [At the same time] you receive the result (outcome, consummation) of your faith....

- 1 Peter 1:8 - 9 (AMP)

As you rejoice, praise and thank God, a bridge is being built between believing and receiving. Just as it takes time to build a bridge in the natural (heavy equipment and durable materials), so it is when you begin to believe God for something He has promised you. Don't give up, but keep on rejoicing and soon you will cross that bridge to your destination. The moment you rejoice in God, Who gave you His promise, is the moment you receive the result or outcome of your faith!

GOD CAN MAKE YOU LAUGH

In the book of Genesis, we find the story of a couple who received a promise from God. Abraham and Sarah were old and well-stricken in age, but God promised them a son in order to establish His eternal covenant. God told Abraham that He was going to bless Sarah, saying, "…I will bless her, and she shall be a mother of nations; kings of people shall be of her" (Gen. 17:16).

When Abraham was 100 years old and Sarah 90, they had the promised miracle child. I like the description Hebrews 11:11 gives: "Through faith also Sarah herself received strength to conceive seed, and was delivered of a child when she was past age, because she judged Him faithful who had promised." Sarah's original laugh of disbelief (Gen. 18:12) was replaced by a laugh of faith. That laugh of faith caused her old body to be rejuvenated and young again. Her womb was changed and made ready to receive the seed from Abraham. She judged God faithful to His promise and laughed until her miracle came. That miracle's name was Isaac, which means laughter. "And Sarah said, God hath made me to laugh, so that all that hear will laugh with me," Gen. 21:6.

> *But let all those that put their trust in thee rejoice....*
> *- Psalm 5:11*

I want to look at something interesting in Abraham and Sarah's story. Most people think only about the conception—the baby—and the miracle itself. But the Holy Ghost is not just interested in the miracle; He's interested in you receiving strength. Sarah received the strength to conceive by faith.

When the Word hits your spirit, like it did with Sarah, conception will occur and you will give birth to your miracle. Laugh at those impossibilities! Laugh in faith! Though Sarah first laughed in unbelief, at some point, she must have started laughing in faith. She must have said, "I'm not the performer; I'm just the believer." And she saw her miracle.

God wants you to know that it's not too late for your miracle today! Believe Him for the impossible, because He specializes in doing amazing miracles even when it seems as if all hope is gone. Romans 4:18 says that Abraham hoped in faith when reason for hope was gone. He must have cheered up as his hope took hold of the faith of God. That hope and cheer came from the Holy Spirit Himself. You can see the action of the Holy Spirit in Romans 15:13: "May the God of your hope so fill you with all joy and peace in believing [through the experience of your faith] that by the power of the Holy Spirit you may abound and be overflowing with hope" (AMP).

Yield to the Holy Spirit's joy and get the strength that you'll need to receive your "Isaac"! Then tell your testimony so that others can rejoice with you.

KEEP YOUR FAITH GOING WITH LAUGHTER

Isaac—the miracle child—followed in his parents' faith and partook of their same blessings. But we see in Genesis 26 that after he had prospered—after he had become great and wealthy—trouble came. The wells which his father Abraham had dug were filled with dirt by the

Philistines. They were stopped up. The same thing often happens after we have been blessed. Satan, who comes to steal, kill, and destroy (John 10:10), fills our "wells" with doubt, fear, sickness, discouragement, distractions, or sin.

Notice what Isaac did. He sent his servants to dig in the valley and they found a well of living water (Gen. 26:19). Unfortunately, nearby herdsmen fought him over it. Undeterred, Isaac kept digging. He had to dig two more wells before finally digging a well called Rehoboth, which means, "the Lord has made room for us and we will be fruitful in the land," (Gen. 26: 22). Isaac just kept on digging wells!

That's what we must do! We must never quit, but with our faith and joy, we need to dig and re-dig those wells of salvation and living water. Isaac (aka Ha, ha, ha) kept the waters of salvation flowing—the same waters his father drank from. He did it with joy!

Demonstrate supernatural joy in your life today by rejoicing, smiling, and laughing. Remember, joy irritates the devil. He likes to hang out in places of depression, grief, and sorrow, but where there is joy the presence and glory of God will come in and run the devil off!

YOU ARE THE BELIEVER — GOD IS THE PERFORMER

When it comes to receiving what you need from God, you are not the performer; you are just the believer. When you see a great athlete or musician play, you praise their ability and enjoy watching them, but there's no pressure on you at all to perform. You're simply enjoying what they produce. It's the same with spiritual things. You do not have to try to produce, or perform, the things the Lord has spoken to you.

Do what you would do if there were no impossibilities. Just as Abraham and Sarah must have put some "action" to their faith in order for Sarah to become pregnant, we must first believe, then act. The only pressure on you is to keep the switch of faith turned on. You do that by believing, speaking, and acting like the Bible is true. Rejoice that what God has promised, He is also able to perform.

That's what Mary, the Mother of Jesus did. When the angel appeared and told her she would give birth to the Son of God, the Bible says she began to praise the Lord. That was her act of faith. "And Mary said, My soul doth magnify the Lord, And my spirit hath rejoiced in God my Savior," Luke 1:46–47. Mary's part was to believe—and she did! Luke 1:45 says, "Blessed is she that believed: for there shall be a performance of those things which were told her from the Lord."

RECEIVING DOORS

One day I went to a furniture store to buy some furniture. I went through the front doors and the displays were very beautiful and inviting. Then I went around to the back to pick up what I had purchased. There I saw a large sign that read, "Receiving." This door was very large and not pretty at all. You could see where trucks had banged into it and there were no fancy lights and colors. It made me think about the place where we receive what we have asked God for. Sometimes it's not very pretty! There's some praising, shouting, singing and dancing going on! While we are doing that, God is backing His "truck" up, unloading healing, answers to prayer, finances or whatever you're believing Him for!

If you'll get happy today—if you'll rejoice—you're going to see a "performance" of what God has promised. Many people never receive their miracle because they never get happy enough to believe "I have it right now. It's mine." Choose to believe, choose to rejoice, and as 1 Peter 1:9 (AMP) says, "...receive the result (outcome, consummation) of your faith."

Remember, the bridge from believing to receiving is joy unspeakable. Your faith does have a beginning, a middle, and an end. In the middle of every faith fight, tell the devil how it is going to turn out. Jesus is the Author and Finisher of your faith, and no matter how bad your situation looks, everything is going to be alright!

Our ultimate goal is Heaven, and along our journey we need to overcome obstacles and win continuous victories. It's like a football team going for the championship. Each week, there's another game—another fight and victory to gain—but the ultimate goal is the championship. So how do you get from the beginning of your faith to the end of it like Peter referred to? Joy is the bridge between believing and receiving. It is a song of praise, a shout of triumph, or even a Holy Ghost dance. Peter called this "joy unspeakable and full of glory" (1 Peter 1:8).

It seemed like a dream, too good to be true, when God returned Zion's exiles. We laughed, we sang, we couldn't believe our good fortune. We were the talk of the nations—"God was wonderful to them!" God was wonderful to us; we are one happy people. And now, God, do it again—bring rains to our drought-stricken lives. So those who planted their crops in despair will shout hurrahs at the harvest, so those who went off with heavy hearts will come home laughing, with armloads of blessing.

Psalm 126 (MSG)

4

Get Ready For a Turn Around

When the Lord turned again the captivity of Zion, we were like them that dream. Then was our mouth filled with laughter, and our tongue with singing: then said they among the heathen, The Lord hath done great things for them. The Lord hath done great things for us; whereof we are glad. Turn again our captivity, O Lord, as the streams in the south. They that sow in tears shall reap in joy. He that goeth forth and weepeth, bearing precious seed, shall doubtless come again with rejoicing, bringing his sheaves with him.

- Psalm 126

God specializes in turning things around! He's been doing it a long time for the nation of Israel. I remember going to Jerusalem in 1970 with my dad on the way to Africa. Our trip happened to coincide with the celebration of the Six Day War of 1967 when Israel defended its borders and gained more territory from Syria. The city that day was filled with great celebration and the area around the Western Wall was the scene of joyous dancing.

In this war, Israel was vastly outnumbered by three countries: Egypt, Syria and Jordan. However, Israel had prepared by rehearsing their strategies of warfare. They attacked from the air and completely overtook the marching military forces of these three nations. Their strategy worked, enabling Israel to gain back territory and increase its borders!

This war was a definite turnaround of a bad situation much like Psalm 126 describes—and the celebration was, too! It's time for a turnaround in your life today! It's time to leave the devil with an overwhelming sense of failure by laughing, dancing and shouting! That's what happens when believers get together to celebrate Christ's victory! Psalm 126:2 says that their mouths were filled with laughter and tongues with singing!

When you see the great victory in Christ on the cross and the resurrection, it will make you laugh! Sometimes in Holy Ghost meetings, you may be rehearsing your plan of attack against the enemy. Our war is not with flesh and blood and our weapons are not natural, but are mighty, supernatural ones. Just as Israel observed the victory of the Six Day War with wonder and amazement, the world looks at the Church and knows that God has done great things for us when our mouths are filled with laughter instead of fear, complaining and worry!

THE GOSPEL BRINGS TURNAROUND

When Jesus came on the scene, He declared that the Spirit of God was upon Him and He was anointed to heal the sick, mend broken hearts and set captives free.

The Spirit of the Lord God is upon me; because the Lord hath anointed me to preach good tidings unto the meek; he hath sent me to bind up the brokenhearted, to proclaim liberty to the captives, and the opening of the prison to them that are bound; To proclaim the acceptable year of the Lord, and the day of vengeance of our God; to comfort all that mourn; To appoint unto them that mourn in Zion, to give unto them beauty for ashes, the oil of joy for mourning, the garment of praise for the

spirit of heaviness; that they might be called trees
of righteousness, the planting of the Lord, that he
might be glorified.
- Isaiah 61:1 - 3

From the first day He was anointed to preach the Gospel – the Good News – Jesus began His mission to turn everything around. Wherever he preached, the results were joy, freedom, and an anointing that destroyed all the works of the devil. Through His death, burial, and resurrection, Christ turned around everything that was lost by Adam's fall. He redeemed mankind from Satan's dominion. That is the Gospel we preach!

The word "gospel" in the Greek is *euangelion*, and means glad tidings, or good news from the battlefield.[1] In the old days, a messenger would be sent from the battlefield to bring the news of a victory, or the gospel.

Today, a battle has been fought and decisively won by Jesus Christ. He triumphed over the enemy, and our job is to tell the good news that a great victory has been won. Wherever this message is heard, there should be some rejoicing going on!

Whenever a wicked, tyrant dictator is hunted down and killed, there is great rejoicing in the streets that can last for many days. The people who have lived in fear are free and the wicked government that controlled their lives is destroyed. This is the message of the Gospel! Our former tyrant dictator—the devil—who controlled us through fear has been destroyed. Jesus Christ is Lord! This is one turnaround celebration that should never end!

GOD LAUGHS AT HIS ENEMIES

> *Why do the heathen rage, and the people imagine a vain thing? The kings of the earth set themselves, and the rulers take counsel together, against the Lord, and against his anointed, saying, Let us break their bands asunder, and cast away their cords from us. He that sitteth in the heavens shall laugh: the Lord shall have them in derision.*
> *- Psalm 2:1 – 4*

Psalm 2 is a picture of God's great plan of redemption. It shows that no evil imagination of Satan to destroy humanity through the demonic manipulation of kings and rulers of nations will ever work. The thief has come to steal, kill and destroy people, but actually he is coming against God.

Remember how Satan worked through kings to kill all the baby boys when both Moses and Jesus were infants?

I can imagine God sitting in the Heavens and laughing at that failed plan. Psalms 2:1-4 also has reference to Revelation 11:18 and Revelation 19:15. These verses refer to the culmination of God's plan of redemption and how He will take care of business in the end times.

Every victory you win in your life is hinged to the great plan of redemption that continues to unfold until Satan is bound. Ephesians 3:10 says, "...now unto principalities and powers in heavenly places might be known by the church the manifold wisdom of God." Your laughing and rejoicing is a sign to the unseen in Heaven and hell, that what God has planned will all come to pass.

The Holy Spirit will prompt you at times, to laugh in derision at the enemy's plans to steal, kill or destroy you. In Christ, you share in His victory procession, "Now thanks be unto God, which always causeth us to triumph in Christ, and maketh manifest the savour of his knowledge by us in every place," 2 Corinthians 2:14. Your laugh of triumph is a sweet smell of victory to Christians and at the same time, defeat to the enemy.

Jesus was betrayed by Judas, abandoned by His friends, beaten and sentenced to death by the Jewish religious and Roman government authorities of that day. Mark 15:1 says the whole council of Jewish scribes, elders, and chief priests held a meeting and decided to destroy Him. What they did fit into the plan spoken by prophets by the inspiration of the Holy Spirit many years before. God got the last laugh when He raised Jesus from the dead! In fact, Paul said that if the princes of this world would have known what was happening when Jesus was crucified, they would have never crucified the Lord of Glory (1 Cor. 2:8).

ENFORCE YOUR AUTHORITY

When you release your authority as a believer, declaring the Word and laughing in derision at your trouble, you are sharing in the victorious power of God over every foe! Acts 4:24-30 is the prayer the church prayed after being persecuted by the Jews for preaching. They quoted Psalm 2 in reference to their trouble that day in prayer. Then they began to praise and magnify God, thankful to be counted worthy to suffer persecution. Jesus had taught them to rejoice when they were persecuted and here was a good opportunity. When they rejoiced, God showed up, shook the place and supplied all their needs! God got the last laugh that day!

Laughing at your enemies such as sickness, poverty, and fear is one way to enforce the authority Jesus gave you. Your enemies are His enemies and you are to tread on serpents, scorpions, and all the power of the enemy (Luke

10:19, Ps. 110:1). Christ's victory is still unfolding. God is the great Judge of all, Who through Christ's work on the cross, has destroyed principalities and powers and made a show of them openly (Col. 2:15). Romans 16:20 says, "And the God of peace shall bruise Satan under your feet shortly...." There is a constant unfolding of the victory won at the cross. When you put the enemy under your feet by laughing in derision you are overcoming. Every battle you win is part of the great plan of redemption that will ultimately see every knee bow and every tongue confess that Jesus is Lord (Phil. 2:10-11).

From Heaven's perspective, there is complete victory! That victory is big enough to cover your situation. Nothing can compare to the triumph of Christ! In view of these facts, we who have been raised to sit with Him in heavenly places, can laugh with Him out of deep respect for His great wisdom and power.

I tell people that if the Almighty God is laughing, you should laugh out of respect, even if you don't understand the joke. If you were with the president of the United States and he told a joke and was laughing, you would laugh with him — even if you didn't understand the joke. How much more should we laugh when God is laughing? He sees the big picture and knows the end from the beginning. He is the God who never says, "uh-oh!" He is never surprised by our situation. He always sees ahead and makes provision for us. Ha, ha, ha! All things work together for good!

GOD TURNS EVIL FOR GOOD

The story of Joseph is a great testimony of the grace of God and of a complete turnaround. When he was still a young boy, his own brothers jealous of how much their father favored him, sold him into slavery. From there, he was promoted, only to be lied about and sent to prison. Instead of becoming bitter, Joseph served with an excellent attitude and came out of prison. He was restored to honor with a new position in the kingdom, new clothes and new influence. After enduring great adversity, Joseph was able to say, "You meant it for evil and God turned it for good" (Gen. 50:20). Everything fit into a plan to save his entire family during a time of famine.

Can you see how your turnaround affects not only you, but generations to come? That is why it's so important to keep on serving God no matter what circumstances you find yourself in. Though you may not realize it at the time, He's working all things together for your good (Rom. 8:28).

God also blessed Joseph with two sons. The first son was named, Manasseh, which means "God made me forget my trouble." Did you know that God can bless you so much you forget your past trouble? God's goodness will turn your depression into a dancing celebration.

Joseph named his next son, Ephraim, which means "God made me fruitful in the land of my affliction." God will make you forget your trouble and He will make you fruitful. God's great favor and grace is available to you today and He is turning your life in a new direction of blessing.

> *Remember ye not the former things, neither consider the things of old. Behold, I will do a new thing; now it shall spring forth; shall ye not know it? I will even make a way in the wilderness, and rivers in the desert.*
> *- Isaiah 43:18 - 19*

God is causing new things to spring forth in your life today, so don't keep dwelling on past failures and mistakes. If Joseph would have dwelled on all his mistreatment, he would have never stepped through the new doors God had before him. You've got to expect God to turn things for you. He is your Father God and He is making a way where there is no way, changing the entire look of your life. He's in the business of turning everything around!

HOW WOULD YOU ACT IF YOU HAD A TURNAROUND?

Hitherto have ye asked nothing in my name: ask,
and ye shall receive, that your joy may be full.

- John 16:24

...and your cup of joy will overflow.

- John 16:24 (TLB)

I have a friend who pastors a great church. He was believing God for three million dollars to build a new auditorium and was very concerned because it was an impossible situation. One day he was trying to pray but was actually worrying and complaining about it to the Lord. He heard the voice of the Holy Spirit ask him in his heart, "How would you act if you already had that money?" He said, "I'd be real happy!" The Lord said, "Well?"

The pastor started praying really hard again and heard the same thing, "How would you act if you had three million dollars?" He replied, "I said I'd be real happy!" Again the Lord said, "Well?" It took that pastor a few times, but he finally got the message and started praising, dancing and shouting like he already had the money. It wasn't long before the entire amount came in!

The next building project my friend started, he went before the Lord again, "Lord, I need 14 million dollars. He heard the Holy Spirit say again, "Well?" This time it didn't take him long to get happy!

He found the secret to answered prayer: "What things soever ye desire when ye pray, believe that ye receive them and ye shall have them," Mark 11:24. "...ask, using my name, and you will receive, and your cup of joy will overflow" (John 16:24, NLB).

Luke 12:32 explains that it is the Father's good pleasure to give you the Kingdom. He wants you to have full joy. So when you pray to the Father in Jesus' name, get your dancing shoes on and begin to act like you've got it! That's your faith in action! Get ready for a turnaround!

IF YOU CAN'T DANCE, JUST SCOOT

Thou hast turned for me my mourning into dancing: thou hast put off my sackcloth, and girded me with gladness.
- Psalm 30:11

When the prodigal son in Luke 15 decided to get up and go home, nothing could stop him. His life began to turn around the moment he stepped toward his father and home. The moment you look away from the hog pen of your situation and believe the Gospel, your situation begins to turn. You are trusting the mercy of God to redeem your life and any time you may have wasted. Something is also happening on God's side. He is ready to give you exceeding abundantly above all you can ask or think (Ephesians 3:20).

The prodigal son's father removed his son's old dirty clothes and cleaned him up. He gave him a new set of clothes and shoes; and placed his ring of authority on his finger (Luke 15:22). Next, he killed a fat calf and threw a party—complete with dancing (vs. 23)!

If you refuse to rejoice in the Lord, you insult the goodness and mercy of God. Just receive that mercy and favor by getting up and putting on your happy party clothes and dancing shoes. I always say, "If you can't dance, just scoot!"

WHEN? TOMORROW AT THIS TIME!

This next story motivates you to go ahead and believe the Word of the Lord even when it seems completely impossible! God has a plan and all things work together for good when you trust and obey Him. I like to say, "God can walk and chew gum at the same time!" Look at these two seemingly unrelated events and how a miracle was performed when someone chose to believe God.

Elisha replied, "Listen to this message from the Lord! This is what the Lord says: By this time tomorrow in the markets of Samaria, five quarts of choice flour will cost only one piece of silver, and ten quarts of barley grain will cost only one piece of silver." The officer assisting the king said to the man of God, "That couldn't happen even if the Lord opened the windows of heaven!" But Elisha replied, "You will see it happen with your own eyes, but you won't be able to eat any of it!"

- 2 Kings 7:1 - 2 (NLT)

BACK AT THE RANCH

I like to watch cowboy movies about the wild west. In these movies I noticed that while the action may have seemed to be in one place, there was always something happening back at the rance. I like to say, while you are rejoicing in one place—something else is happening in another place!

In the story of Elisha, something was happening "back at the ranch." The story goes that there were four lepers having a heyday eating all kinds of food and finding clothes and treasures left behind by the army. They were laughing, shouting, eating, and looting until they started feeling guilty about all the people starving in the city. This was like a dream come true. It was too good to keep it to themselves, so they quickly went back with the good news of all the food and goods abandoned by their enemies. After checking to make sure it wasn't a trap, all of Samaria began running toward the Aramean's camp to get in on the feast and treasures. I like the rest of the story. The king's officer, who had not believed the prophet, was sitting at the gate and got trampled to death, just as the prophet Elisha said (2 Kings 7:1-7, 20).

When anyone believes the Word of God, they will see the glory of God. Elisha believed God—and provision was made "back at the ranch."

WHAT TO DO WHEN YOU GET A TURNAROUND

From beginning to end, the Bible is full of turnarounds. Jesus went everywhere preaching the Good News and turning impossible situations around. He turned funerals into celebrations, water into wine, a stoning to a transformed life and sickness into joy and health. The Apostle Peter experienced several supernatural turnarounds himself. He found tax money in a fish's mouth, forgiveness, Pentecostal power and an angelic midnight jail break! That's why he could rejoice with joy unspeakable and full of glory even in the darkest fiery trial. "Yet believing, ye rejoice with joy unspeakable and full of glory," 1 Peter 1:8.

Here are some things to remember when you have a prophetic word but the situation seems impossible: 1) Don't doubt, just shout and God will work it all out. 2) It doesn't take long for a turnaround. 3) When you experience a turnaround, don't keep it to yourself, but tell others about it. God not only has your need in mind, but your act of faith might cause a whole family, city, or nation to rejoice and change.

Rejoice! It's never too late for a turnaround and dreams can come true. Rejoice! The Lord has done great things for you. "Then was our mouth filled with laughter, and our tongue with singing: then said they among the heathen, The Lord hath done great things for them. The Lord hath done great things for us; whereof we are glad," Psalm 126:2-3. It's time to rejoice, because your turnaround can turn a generation!

1 Meares, Aaron, diligentsoul.wordpress.com

Some of the most serious

business of Heaven is

conducted in an

atmosphere of JOY.

5

Taking Care of Business

Joy is the serious business of Heaven.

- C. S. Lewis

For the kingdom of God is not meat and drink; but righteousness, and peace, and joy in the Holy Ghost.

- Romans 14:17

I love this quote from C.S. Lewis, a respected author who had some great things to say about joy. He said, "Joy is the serious business of Heaven." [1] In other words, Heaven conducts its most serious business in an atmosphere of joy. In the Kingdom of God, there is some business being taken care of! While you rejoice, transactions are made and prayers answered. People may warn, "You better take this situation seriously!" When you apply the blood of Jesus and then rejoice, you can tell them, "I am taking this extremely serious!"

My mother used to "take care of business" by shouting and running around the church. My dad would comment as she ran, "It's not necessary unless it's necessary!" Is it necessary? Yes! If God sits in the Heavens and laughs until He sees all His enemies under His feet, then we the Church, citizens of His Kingdom, should take our place in Christ and conduct Kingdom business with Him in an atmosphere of victory, knowing the good work God has begun, He will finish!

> *He that sitteth in the heavens shall laugh....*
> *- Psalm 2:4*

> *And hath raised us up together, and made us sit together in heavenly places in Christ Jesus.*
> *- Ephesians 2:6*

When the Body of Christ meets together, it is for the purpose of worshipping God and "taking care of business." I like what William Barclay says about the church.

> *The Greek word for Church is ecclesia and was originally used to describe a gathering of the citizens of Athens. Its decisions conformed to the laws of the state and its powers were to all intents and purposes unlimited. It declared war, made peace, contracted treaties and arranged alliances. It was ultimately responsible for the conduct of all military operations. It raised and allocated funds. It comes from the Hebrew root word which means "to summon." In the Hebrew sense it means God's people being called together to listen to or act for God.* [2]
>
> *William Barclay*
> *New Testament Words*

The book of Acts emphasizes the place where they were assembled was shaken. There is always "some assembly required" for the power of God to shake the earth. (Acts 4:31). There was a corporate prayer meeting and a corporate faith as they lifted their voices together.

Hebrews 4:16 tells us what we'll find at the throne of

grace when we come boldly by the blood. We can obtain mercy and find grace to help us in the time of need. Then we take our place in a great assembly of the Body of Christ in Heaven and earth and participate in Heaven's business carried out in the earth.

> *But ye are come unto mount Sion, and unto the city of the living God, the heavenly Jerusalem, and to an innumerable company of angels, To the general assembly and church of the firstborn, which are written in heaven, and to God the Judge of all, and to the spirits of just men made perfect, And to Jesus the mediator of the new covenant, and to the blood of sprinkling, that speaketh better things than that of Abel.*
>
> *- Hebrews 12:22 - 24*

God the Father is on the throne with Jesus seated at His right hand. Angels with eyeballs all around their heads, circle about them. (I used to think my mom had those eyeballs in church. I couldn't get away with anything!)

What is the business that Heaven, earth, angels, God, and Jesus are taking care of? The business of the kingdom is to enforce all that Jesus bought for the Church at the cross. God is using the Church to display His wisdom to principalities and powers. Paul called that wisdom foolishness to the world (1 Corinthians 1:21). Remember, Heaven conducts its most serious business in an atmosphere of joy. The atmosphere of joy releases power to do miracles. It will destroy the works of darkness until that day when the God of Peace forever crushes Satan underneath our feet (Rom. 16:20). We live in the consciousness of the triumph of Christ. We are the triumphant Church!

My dad's church knew how to take care of business. A prophecy or message from God would be declared and then, there would be great joy in the Holy Ghost! I used to wonder what was going on! Now I know that needs were being met, bodies were being healed, and the joy of the Lord was mending broken hearts! That's what happens when the church comes together. There can be a song, prophecy, tongue or revelation. When people believe the Word of God that comes forth, they can receive it with joy unspeakable and full of glory! I call that "gathering the spoil." It is the Kingdom culture.

GATHER UP THE SPOIL

You [O Lord] have multiplied the nation and increased their joy; they rejoice before You like the joy in harvest, as men rejoice when they divide the spoil [of battle].

- Isaiah 9:3 (AMP)

Therefore will I divide Him a portion with the great [kings and rulers], and He shall divide the spoil with the mighty, because He poured out His life unto death....

- Isaiah 53:12 (AMP)

Something very powerful happens in times of rejoicing. It is not simply emotionalism, but it is people believing the Gospel and receiving all that Jesus purchased in His redemptive work on the cross.

David said in Psalm 119:162, "I rejoice at thy word, as one that findeth great spoil." What exactly is a spoil? *Noah Webster's 1828 Dictionary* defines spoil as: goods or possessions taken; particularly in war; that which is gained by strength. [3]

Jesus, through death, entered hell itself and took back all that Adam lost in the fall. Colossians 2:15 says, "And having spoiled principalities and powers, he made a shew of them openly, triumphing over them in it." The *Noli* translation says, "He despoiled the infernal dominions and realms. He dragged their rulers as captives in procession, and through his cross he led us all to triumph." <u>The</u> <u>Twentieth Century New Testament</u> reads, "He rid himself of all the Powers of Evil, and held them up to open contempt when he celebrated his triumph over them on the cross!" What is happening when someone hears the Gospel and believes it? That is called "gathering up the spoil!"

In His redemptive work, prophesied by Isaiah, Jesus divided the spoil of the greatest battle ever fought and won in the history of mankind! What are some of the spoils of the battle that Christ won? Salvation, health, prosperity, peace, restoration in marriages and families, and a great harvest of souls.

If you only knew what happens in the spirit when you rejoice, you would rejoice every day! You're gathering up the spoils! Isaiah 53:12 says that Jesus divides the spoil of the battle with the strong. The joy of the Lord is your strength. So when you rejoice, the power of God is strengthening you to enforce Christ's victory and win in every battle you face.

> *I rejoice at thy word, as one that findeth great spoil.*
> - *Psalm 119:162*

When you hear or read the Word, there is a proper response. David rejoiced as one who found great spoil and you should act like you would if you found a million dollars. When you respond with joyful praise, you are gathering the spoil!

JOY IN HARVEST

The Word promises that those who sow in tears shall reap in joy (Ps. 126:5). Joy is a harvesting machine. Harvest time is a time for ACTION. You've prayed, you've believed and now it is time to reap with JOY!

Look closely at 1 Peter 1:8 - 9: "Whom having not seen, ye love; in whom, though now ye see him not, yet believing, ye rejoice with joy unspeakable and full of glory: Receiving the end of your faith, even the salvation of your souls." The focus of your attention is Jesus, whom you love and have faith in. Because you believe Him and His Word, you rejoice with "heavenly, triumphant joy" that is a container of the glory of God. When you rejoice, you receive! Rejoicing is a sign that what you have believed for is done and that you are reaping the harvest of your faith! Get ready to see the glory of God!

When Adam sinned, he lost the divine splendor and dominion man was created to have. Because of our identification with Adam, all have sinned and come short of the glory of God (Rom. 3:23). Through Christ, however, God has brought His children back into glory. The work of redemption was a restoration of the glory of God!

For it became him, for whom are all things, and by whom are all things, in bringing many sons unto glory, to make the captain of their salvation perfect through sufferings.

- Hebrews 2:10

WHAT IS IN THE GLORY?

Let's look at what is contained in the Glory. Here is the description of the word glory that I wrote down years ago from a Bible commentary. Glory contains wealth, numbers, commerce, power, wisdom, promotion, superiority, dignity, authority, nobility, splendor, valor, magnificence, extraordinary privileges and advantages. According to proper Bible interpretation and the "Law of First Mention," the first time a word is used in the scriptures, and every time thereafter, it must include the same simple and original meaning. It doesn't have to be the only meaning, but it must include the original meaning first. The first reference to glory in the Bible is found in

Genesis 31:1 and refers to the wealth of Jacob. Therefore any other time the word glory is used in the Bible it also includes wealth.

All of these words are descriptive of those who are taking care of business. There's commerce, numbers, promotion, etc. in the glory! Paul said God would supply all your need according to His riches in glory. You can see that the atmosphere of Heaven is found in the glory and there is no lack in Heaven!

The church in the book of Acts knew how to access that realm through the preaching of the Gospel, unified prayer and being filled with the Holy Ghost. Every need was met by the spirit of generosity (Acts 2:45; 4:34, 35). Even when they were persecuted, they would call a prayer meeting and before it was over, the Holy Ghost would fall. They would be filled with joy in the Holy Ghost and every need would be supplied.

Rejoicing is a pipeline to the glory of God! Keep the pipeline open and flowing every day and stay tapped into the supply of Heaven for your house. "Rejoice in the Lord always: and again I say, Rejoice," Phil. 4:4. Rejoicing and the glory of God always go together. Joy ushers in the glory and brings you into His Presence. In the Lord's Presence is fullness of joy (Ps. 16:11), and all of His goodness – in every facet of His being. God is a good God!

I've got good news for you. Jesus has gone to Heaven, but He sent the Holy Spirit so we can have the glory of Heaven here in the Earth. It is the joy of the Lord!

TRANSFORMED BY THE GLORY OF GOD

> *But we all, with open face beholding as in a glass the glory of the Lord, are changed into the same image from glory to glory, even as by the Spirit of the Lord.*
>
> *- 2 Corinthians 3:18*

> *And all of us, as with unveiled face, [because we] continued to behold [in the Word of God] as in a mirror the glory of the Lord, are constantly being transfigured into His very own image in ever increasing splendor and from one degree of glory to another; [for this comes] from the Lord [Who is] the Spirit.*
>
> *- 2 Corinthians 3:18 (AMP)*

In Luke's Gospel, Jesus went up a mountain to pray with three of his disciples. As He prayed, something happened that impacted them – something they would never forget. They saw a transformation take place in

Christ and they beheld His glory (Luke 9:32). Jesus was shining so brightly that His clothes were glistening white!

This is the same Christ Paul saw on the road to Damascus – the One Who changed Him forever! John, another of Jesus' disciples, also experienced the glory and wrote, "And the Word was made flesh, and dwelt among us, (and we beheld his glory, the glory as of the only begotten of the Father,) full of grace and truth," John 1:14. Even when he was on the isle of Patmos, John never forgot this glory. It continued to unfold before him – the revelation of Christ. Just like these men, when we rejoice with joy unspeakable we are filled and transformed by the glory of God.

There's something about the Presence of God that brings a satisfaction and joy that can be found in no other thing in this earth. It is a tangible substance called glory and it comes from Heaven.

Whenever someone tells or hears the Gospel of Christ, the glory of God shows up. By the time the Holy Spirit is finished working, people are filled with God's love and peace. Healing and grace are manifested as every need is met! There is something called joy! I call it "taking care of business!" Ha, ha, ha! Get to laughing, because Heaven does conducts its most serious business in an atmosphere of joy!

And He walks with me; and He talks with me;

And He tells me I am His own.

And the joy we share as we tarry there;

None other has ever known. [4]

1 Lewis, C. (2002). *Letters to Malcolm. New York, NY: Harcourt, Inc.*

2 Barclay, W. *New Testament Words. Louisville, KY: Westminister John Knox Press.*

3 Dictionary, *Noah Webster's 1828 American. (n.d.). Retrieved December 2011, from www.1828-dictionary.com.*

4 Miles, C. A. (1912, March). *In The Garden. (C. A. Miles, Performer).*

This is the day which the Lord hath made; we will

rejoice and be glad in it.

- Psalm 118:24

This is the day of the Lord's victory; let us be happy,

let us celebrate!

- GNTD

This is the very day God acted - let's

celebrate and be festive!

- MSG

This is the day which the Lord has brought about; we

will rejoice and be glad in it.

- AMP

6

The Time of Our Joy

*If you only knew what happens in the spirit when
you rejoice, you would rejoice every day!*
- Mark Hankins

Under the Old Covenant there were certain procedures
to follow on the Day of Atonement. One of the sacrifices
made on the Day of Atonement involved two goats. The
first goat was sacrificed in the temple and its blood was
applied to the mercy seat. The other goat, the scapegoat,
was led into the wilderness. The following are excerpts
from the book, <u>*The Holy Temple of Jerusalem*</u>, by Chaim
Richman. I like how this book describes what happened

on the Day of Atonement and the celebration—the time of joy—that followed.

> *The high priest then tied a length of crimson-dyed wool between the horns of the scapegoat and tied a similar length of wool around the neck of the goat that was to be sacrificed. The wool was dyed crimson in accordance with the verse, "...though your sins be as scarlet, they shall be as white as snow; though they be red like crimson, they shall be as wool" (Isaiah 1:18).*
>
> *Arriving at the cliff, the priest removed the crimson wool that the high priest had tied to the scapegoat's horns. He divided it into two pieces, tying one to the animal's horns and the second to a rock so that he would be able to see when the crimson color had turned white and know that atonement had been made for Israel's sins. Then he pushed the goat backward with his two hands.*
>
> *After he had accomplished his task, the priest who had led the scapegoat walked back to the last booth, and waited there until dark before he returned to Jerusalem – for he had only been permitted to travel this distance in order to fulfill the duty of the scapegoat. After having given the scapegoat to*

his colleague, the High Priest had to wait until he received word that the scapegoat had reached the desert, and thus he could precede to the next stage of the day's service. In addition to the crimson wool on the Sanctuary miraculously turning white, this information reached the temple another way. Scouts were positioned at high points all along the route to the cliff and, as the goat was led from one station to the next, these scouts would signal to each other by waving cloths, and when the scapegoat had finally been cast off, the news was relayed back to the temple through the scouts' signal. [1]

Just as the children of Israel rejoiced over the blood, we can rejoice when we understand what the blood of Christ has done for us. Thank God, the blood of Jesus has been applied once for all time, once for all conditions, once for all men, and once for all blessing. Hebrews 9:12 says, "Neither by the blood of goats and calves, but by his own blood he entered in once into the holy place, having obtained eternal redemption for us." We are redeemed children of God.

When the Gospel is preached today, you can look at the faces and responses of those who hear the message and tell who truly believe. Those who understand will respond with joy and praise, dancing, and thanksgiving. Years ago, in old-time spirit-filled gatherings, when people were filled with joy and the Holy Ghost they would take out their handkerchiefs and begin to wave them, signaling that they had the victory. This was a demonstration of joy and celebration.

Just like those saints, just like those scouts in the Old Testament, let us signal to one another, telling the glorious message that though our sins were as scarlet, they are now as white as snow. Though they were red like crimson, they are now as wool (Isaiah 1:18)!

Believers frequently quote Psalm 118:24 when they are referring to rejoicing in the Lord – each and every day – and that's good. However, this is actually a prophetic scripture that joyfully anticipates the coming Messiah. Jesus used it to refer to Himself in the work of redemption in John 8:56, "Abraham rejoiced to see my day: and he saw it, and was glad." In the Old Testament, the people joyfully looked forward to the great day when the Messiah would come. Now, we can look back at God's work of redemption and we rejoice and are glad. We also joyfully anticipate the Messiah's second coming.

THE REVERENT AND WISE REJOICE

After the sacrifice had been accepted, it was time for the Festival of Tabernacles, which was also known as "the time of our joy." The rejoicing took place mainly in the Holy Temple, the central point of Jewish worship.

> *And ye shall take you on the first day the boughs of goodly trees, branches of palm trees, and the boughs of thick trees, and willows of the brook; and ye shall rejoice before the Lord your God seven days. And ye shall keep it a feast unto the Lord seven days in the year. It shall be a statute forever in your generations: ye shall celebrate it in the seventh month. Ye shall dwell in booths seven days; all that are Israelites born shall dwell in booths. That your generations may know that I made the children of Israel to dwell in booths, when I brought them out of the land of Egypt: I am the Lord your God.*
> *- Leviticus 23:40 - 43*

After the sacrifice was accepted, the children of Israel were commanded to rejoice for seven days. Even the smartest and most influential men in that generation rejoiced and celebrated because they understood what the blood had done.

Some have accused those who exhibit great joy and rejoicing as being ignorant or foolish. However it is the wisdom of God. I like how Proverbs describes the rejoicing nature of wisdom, "Then I [Wisdom] was beside Him as a master and director of the work; and I was daily His delight, rejoicing before Him always," Proverbs 8:30 (AMP).

At the foot of Mount Moriah, in the City of David, there is a natural spring called Siloam, the source of Jerusalem's water. As it is located literally in the shadow of the Holy Temple, it has always had spiritual significance for Israel.

Each day of the festival, the priest went down to Siloam Temple. There, they filled a golden flask with three lug (about ½ liter) of the pure water and returned to the Temple through the West Gate, on the southern side of the court. As they entered the gate, their steps were greeted by the sound of trumpets and shofar blasts, in fulfillment of the prophet's words, "Therefore with joy shall ye draw water out of the wells of salvation" (Isaiah 12:3).

The actual participants in the celebration were not the common folk, but the greatest scholars and the

most pious men of the generation – the heads of the
Sanhedrin, the sages, the academy heads, and the
elders. In the presence of all those assembled in
the Holy Temple, these exceedingly righteous men
would dance, sing, and rejoice. [1]

These exceedingly righteous men had knowledge and understanding of the blood sacrifices and wine libations together. They had reason to rejoice because they knew these celebrations signified the fulfilling of Isaiah 12:3, which is a type of salvation we receive through Jesus Christ. They were commanded to rejoice because their sins were covered for one year.

Under the New Covenant, we rejoice because our sins have been remitted eternally when we believe and receive what Jesus has done for us in redemption. We have been made the very righteousness of God and we should be glad!

But let the righteous be glad; let them rejoice before
God: yea, let them exceedingly rejoice.
- Psalm 68:3

We also rejoice because the blood has been shed and the enemy has been defeated! Psalm 27:6 says, "And now shall mine head be lifted up above mine enemies round about me: therefore will I offer in his tabernacle sacrifices of joy; I will sing, yea, I will sing praises unto the Lord."

We have a spring of living water continually flowing and bubbling within us (John 4:14)—the same water that Jesus spoke of to the woman at the well (John 4:13). That means we can worship the Father in spirit and in truth — anytime, anywhere.

EXCESSIVE CELEBRATION

In the game of football, the goal is to make a touchdown. The player who does this sometimes goes into quite a demonstration of joy! He might do his own personal dance or shout to celebrate, which is fine, but if you go a little too long the officials will blow their whistles and give you a penalty for "excessive celebration." When we rejoice before the Lord, remembering all He has accomplished in our redemption, He does not throw a flag and penalize us for excessive rejoicing! In fact, He joins in! Zephaniah 3:17 says, "The LORD thy God in the midst of thee is mighty; he will save, he will rejoice over thee with joy; he will rest in his love, he will joy over thee with singing."

Truly reverent people will break forth into excessive, exceeding, great joy as Philippians 4:4 instructs us to "Rejoice in the Lord always: and again I say, rejoice." That is what the Kingdom is all about: righteousness, and peace, and joy in the Holy Ghost (Rom. 14:17). First Peter 1:8 says, "Whom having not seen, ye love; in whom, though ye see Him not, yet believing, ye rejoice with joy unspeakable and full of glory." Heaven's joy is full of glory!

THE PRESENCE OF GOD BRINGS BLESSING

When David became king, he desired to bring the Ark of the Covenant back to Jerusalem. His first attempt was met with disappointment because the Ark wasn't carried on the priest's shoulders and accompanied with joy. David left it in the house of Obed-Edom and God's blessing began to come on that household (2 Sam. 6:11).

In 2 Samuel 6, we read how David again went to get the Ark. This time he brought it to Jerusalem with much joy and dancing, and sacrifices. Every six paces, he stopped to offer a blood sacrifice (vs. 13). The glory of the Lord began to fall on their company until David danced with all his might (vs. 14) and the entire house of Israel brought up the Ark with shouting and with the sound of the trumpet. All this happened in the Old Testament.

Today, we live under a new and better Covenant and because of the blood of Jesus – our bodies are the temple of the Holy Ghost. We have left the type and the shadow and are now living in the reality of righteousness and the very presence of God within us. That means you can put your faith in the blood of Jesus, believe, and then rejoice because healing, deliverance and financial blessing have already been provided. As you release your faith and rejoice – as you begin to sing and dance – the glory of God will fill you to overflowing. The Holy Spirit will take the triumph of Christ and make it real to you. You will then experience the power of the Living Water from Heaven.

> *Therefore with joy shall ye draw water out of the wells of salvation.*
> *- Isaiah 12:3*

You can make a withdrawal from your salvation account with joy. The wells of salvation are reservoirs of healing and blessing. Joy is your bucket to draw much salvation. If you have great joy, you have a great bucket to draw much salvation.

Those reservoirs and wells of salvation are not just for you, they are for whoever is thirsty. In John 7, Jesus said when He was celebrating this feast in Jerusalem, as He observed crowds of thirsty religious Jews around Him, is anybody thirsty? Is anyone tired of the dry traditions and rituals? Come to me and drink! He said all you must do is believe. "He that believeth on me, as the scriptures hath said, out of his belly shall flow rivers of living water," John 7:38. On the day of Pentecost, the Holy Spirit was poured out on the early church. They began to drink from the heavenly wells of salvation and the results were joy unspeakable. These deep wells of salvation truly satisfy and began on that day as the church spoke with tongues and magnified God. They were changed by the Holy Spirit and filled with faith.

Faith in what God has done demands a response. For exceedingly righteous people, the proper response is to rejoice! You may not feel like rejoicing, but do it anyway. Joy is a fruit of the spirit and every fruit will crucify your flesh. As you make the choice to rejoice you'll experience and enjoy all that Jesus' blood purchased for you.

Choose to be like the truly righteous men of old who weren't afraid to dance and rejoice before the Lord. The very presence of the Holy Spirit, the water, and the wine from Heaven is poured into your heart, and it's like nothing the world can bring! Respond appropriately with expressions of heavenly, triumphant joy – just as God's people were commanded to do for a week in the Old Covenant. You can experience such joy when you believe the Gospel! Drink the living water of the Holy Spirit. Rejoice and celebrate your victory in the blood of Jesus!

1 Richman, C. (1997). *The Holy Temple of Jerusalem*. Jerusalem, Israel: Carta.

And I will ask the Father, and He will give you another

Comforter (Counselor, Helper, Intercessor, Advocate,

Strengthener, and Standby) that He may remain with

you forever—The Spirit of Truth, Whom the world

cannot receive (welcome, take to its heart), because it

does not see Him or know and recognize Him. But

you know and recognize Him, for He lives with you

[constantly] and will be in you.

- John 14:16 - 17 (AMP)

But the fruit of the Spirit is love, joy, peace,

longsuffering, gentleness, goodness, faith, meekness,

temperance: against such there is no law.

- Galatians 5:22 - 23

7

Yield To the Holy Spirit

A pastor of a great church was attending a meeting where the Holy Spirit was moving and people around him were responding with laughter, shouting and praising. He was just standing there observing and analyzing everything when the minister walked up to him and said, "Why don't you yield to the Holy Spirit?"

He thought, "Yield. Hmmm, that's an interesting concept." He pulled out his Greek Lexicon from his pocket and looked up the word. In the Greek the word yield refers to when a soldier presents himself to his commanding officer for orders. After seeing this, he realized that he needed to respond to the Person of the Holy Spirit and follow the impulses he was given by the Holy Spirit to laugh, dance, and shout for joy. The Holy Spirit will prompt you to rejoice at the most unusual times. He takes what Christ has done *FOR* us and makes it real *IN* us!

As we yield to the Holy Spirit, we will become familiar with the "way of the Spirit" which brings the power of joy to any situation. In John 14:16-17, Jesus introduced the Holy Spirit to His disciples as the Comforter. I like to read these verses in *The Amplified Bible*. The Bible gives a good description of who the Holy Spirit is and what He does in and for us.

> *And I will ask the Father, and He will give you another Comforter (Counselor, Helper, Intercessor, Advocate, Strengthener, and Standby) that He may remain with you forever — The Spirit of Truth, Whom the world cannot receive (welcome, take to its heart), because it does not see Him or know and recognize Him. But you know and recognize Him, for He lives with you [constantly] and will be in you.*
> *- John 14:16 - 17 (AMP)*

Notice verse 17 says He will be in you. Who is this Holy Spirit who lives in you? What is He doing? The

Greek word for Comforter here is "Parakletos." Dr. P.C. Nelson, a Greek and Hebrew scholar who was fluent in 32 different languages and who wrote a book of fundamental Bible doctrines said the Greek word Parakletos actually means: Advocate, Counselor, and Intercessor. He went on to say that the "Advocate/Counselor" is called in for His excellence in three areas: 1) His exceptional knowledge 2) His expertise in protocol and procedure 3) His persuasive speaking ability. [1] When the Holy Spirit is working on your case, you have a tremendous advantage because He has a reputation for winning cases. I love what my dad, B.B. Hankins said, **"The Holy Spirit is a genius; if you listen to Him he will make you look smart."**

He may prompt you to praise, laugh, shout, sing, or say a scripture out loud. He can come gushing out of your belly like a mighty river of joy and shouting. He'll remind you of the victory won in redemption and that if God is for you, then who can be against you (Rom. 8:31)! It may be proper protocol and procedure to apply the blood of Jesus and then dance in the Presence of Jehovah Rapha until healing is manifested in your body. No matter what He prompts you to do, listen to the Comforter – the Counselor – within. He will fill you with joy that not only gives you strength but also brings in the glory of God!

UNCOMMON STRENGTH

William Barclay, another Bible scholar, describes the work of the "Parakletos" this way: "The kind of comfort and consolation in distress which keeps a man on his feet, when, left to himself, he would collapse. It is the comfort, which enables a man or woman to pass the breaking point and not to break. He is one who is called in to help in a situation with which a man by himself cannot cope. He exhorts men to high deeds and noble thoughts." [2]

The prayer of the Apostle Paul in Ephesians 3:14 - 21 describes the kind of strength the Holy Spirit supplies in the inner man of every believer.

> *May He grant you out of the rich treasury of His glory to be strengthened and reinforced with mighty power in the inner man by the [Holy] Spirit [Himself indwelling your innermost being and personality].*
> - *Ephesians 3:16 (AMP)*

The Holy Spirit strengthens us with mighty power, fills us with the fullness of God, and does exceeding, abundantly above all we can ask or think!

We have a friend who pastors a great church. The

church also runs a school and this pastor is the coach of the girl's basketball team. In one particular game, this pastor's team was losing terribly. They were making silly mistakes and by half-time, were very discouraged.

Our friend, the coach, took the team back to the locker room at half-time. He was planning to fire them up by chewing them out. Instead, he sensed the Holy Spirit giving him some "expertise in speaking ability and knowledge"—exactly what he needed at that moment. He gathered the girls close and told them to think about all the mistakes they had made—how they had missed baskets and made fouls, etc. Then he told them to laugh at those mistakes! Now that was unusual! But it worked! The girls got to laughing so much that they forgot their frustration and went out in the second half and won the game! Not only that, but they went on to take the state championship that year! The Holy Ghost knows how to win in anything—even basketball!

Rev. Kenneth Hagin (Dad Hagin) tells the story about his face being paralyzed on one side. He went to church and had hands laid on him for healing. There were no visible changes after he got home, but he said, "When hands were laid on me, I believe I received my healing!" His friends were puzzled and argued with him because he still looked the same after prayer.

That night he laid down to sleep, but couldn't doze off because one eye stayed open. He said he decided to praise God for healing him and just laughed in his bed for four or five hours. As he did, he finally fell asleep. He woke up completely healed! The Holy Ghost prompted him to laugh and strengthened him to believe. Then the glory of God quickened his body, perfectly restoring him. I call that excellence in procedure!

EXCEPTIONAL KNOWLEDGE AND SPEAKING ABILITY

But as it is written: "Eye has not seen, nor ear heard, nor have entered into the heart of man the things which God has prepared for those who love Him." But God has revealed them to us through His Spirit. For the Spirit searches all things, yes, the deep things of God. For what man knows the things of a man except the spirit of the man which is in him? Even so no one knows the things of God except the Spirit of God. Now we have received, not the spirit of the world, but the Spirit who is from God, that we might know the things that have been freely given to us by God. These things we also speak, not in words which man's wisdom teaches but which the Holy Spirit teaches, comparing spiritual things with spiritual. But the natural man does not receive the things of the Spirit of God, for they are foolishness to him; nor can he know them, because they are spiritually discerned.

- *1 Corinthians 2:9 - 14 (NKJV)*

On the day of Pentecost, after being "drunk in the Holy Ghost" and having great joy, Peter stood up and preached with such eloquence and exceptional knowledge that it had to be the Holy Spirit helping him! Three thousand people were saved (Acts 2)! That's not bad for a rough fisherman!

On the way to prayer in Acts 3, Peter and John were already so full of boldness that they commanded the crippled man at the Beautiful Gate to get up and walk. He did and then started running around the place, leaping and shouting (vs. 8)! That is powerful speaking ability!

Great boldness, ability, and joy are not "natural" but supernatural and get supernatural results. Peter did not get up and say, "I'm Peter, you know, the one who denied Jesus. I'm so ashamed. I don't know what I'm doing here. I don't deserve it. Yes, I denied Jesus—not once, not twice, but three times! I even thought about going to hang out with Judas. And that little chicken...I wanted to wring his little, skinny neck! He crowed on and on." (That's why I say preachers like chicken so much.)

No! Peter didn't even mention his failure. Nowadays, most religious people would never let him forget his trouble, let alone get up and preach without going through years of rehab. But when Peter was filled with the Holy Ghost and joy, he wasn't afraid or ashamed any longer. Instead, he was bold, full of joy, and counted worthy to suffer persecution for Jesus' sake (Acts 5:41).

No matter what you've done today, no matter what others have said or done to you, the blood of Jesus completely cleanses you from sin and restores you to fellowship with God. Let's look at David. As soon as he repented of his sin, there was restoration of joy in the Holy Spirit. Here is his prayer:

> *Create in me a clean heart, O God; and renew a right spirit within me. Cast me not away from thy presence; and take not thy holy spirit from me. Restore unto me the joy of thy salvation; and uphold me with thy free spirit.*
> *Psalm 51:10 - 12*

WHAT TO DO WHEN YOU MESS UP

One of my grandsons, Jude, was in the middle of being potty trained and was getting ready to start preschool. In preschool, the children all have to be able to take care of themselves in the area of going to the bathroom. That's when their parents start getting really serious about this stage of development! Jude was having some challenges in this area and I noticed one day when he was playing at my house that he had gotten real quiet. I've learned when children get quiet you'd better look for them.

I noticed Jude was standing over in the drapes, real still. I said, "Jude, what are you doing? Did you mess in your britches?" He didn't say anything. "Jude, come here. Come to Poppy." He walked to me, his legs stretched out, awkwardly walking to me. I then called for some assistance from his mother, because taking care that kind of business is definitely out of my department!

I got to thinking that this is how Christians act when they've "messed up" in some area of their Christian life. Maybe they quit going to church or got into sin and they're out somewhere—"hiding in the drapes!" You call them, asking if something is wrong. Of course, they deny it or make some excuses. When, after some coaxing, they open up and start coming to talk to you, they are walking like

Jude walked when he messed his britches! They repent and the Lord cleans them up. They become happy again, and get right back in the middle of church with all the rest of the believers.

The power of the blood of Jesus continually cleanses us from all unrighteousness. Even the smell of sin is gone and there is a refreshing of the Holy Spirit!

We cannot enjoy life when we know we've sinned and missed the mark. God doesn't leave us in a hopeless condition, but has made a way for us to be restored. We can come boldly to the throne of grace to find mercy for our failures and grace to meet our needs.

> *Having therefore, brethren, boldness to enter into the holiest by the blood of Jesus.*
> *- Hebrews 10:19*

> *But if we walk in the light, as he is in the light, we have fellowship one with another, and the blood of Jesus Christ his Son cleanseth us from all sin. If we confess our sins, he is faithful and just to forgive us our sins, and to cleanse us from all unrighteousness.*
> *- 1 John 1:7, 9*

Today, the blood of Jesus completely cleanses from sin and all unrighteousness and restores fellowship with God and joy in the Holy Ghost. As Smith Wigglesworth said, "There is not one thing in me the blood does not cleanse." I like to say, "Where the blood flows, the Holy Ghost goes!" Instead of having a nervous breakdown, get up—shout, dance and rejoice and give the devil a nervous breakdown instead!

[1] *Nelson, P. (29th Printing 2007). Bible Doctrines. Springfield, MO: Gospel Publishing House.*

[2] *Barclay, W. New Testament Words. Louisville, KY: Westminister John Knox Press.*

Happy are those who hear the joyful call to worship,

for they will walk in the light of your presence, Lord.

They rejoice all day long in your wonderful reputation.

They exult in your righteousness.

- Psalm 89:15 - 16 (NLT)

This day is holy to God. Don't feel bad. The joy of

God is your strength!

- Nehemiah 8:10 (MSG)

The Holy Spirit prompts us to rejoice so we can be

filled with Him. Why do you have to be continually

filled with the Holy Spirit? Because you leak!

- Mark Hankins

8

Proper Protocol Is Joy

I have a friend who is a very successful businessman. I was eating dinner with him one night and he told me that he had a sign in his office that read, "You have ten seconds to get enthusiastic or get out of my office!" When you come in his office, you had better be excited about taking care of business.

How much more we should wake up every day go into the throne room of grace with joy and anticipation to have a meeting with God and then go out to do "kingdom business." King David said, "Make a joyful noise unto the Lord, all ye lands. Serve the Lord with gladness: Come before His presence with singing...Enter into His gates with thanksgiving and into his courts with praise, be thankful unto Him, and bless His name" (Psalm 100:1, 2, 4). Now that is the proper protocol for entering the presence of God. It is enthusiastic.

> *And my language and my message were not set forth in persuasive (enticing and plausible) words of wisdom, but they were in demonstration of the [Holy] Spirit and power [a proof by the Spirit and power of God, operating on me and stirring in the minds of my hearers the most holy emotions and thus persuading them], So that your faith might not rest in the wisdom of men (human philosophy), but in the power of God.*
>
> *- 1 Corinthians 2:4 – 5 (AMP)*

I found it very interesting that <u>*The Merriam-Webster Dictionary's*</u> first definition for enthusiasm is "belief in special revelation of the Holy Spirit." [1] In both the Latin and Greek the origin of enthusiasm mean "a possession by God or having God within." [2] In the 1650's the Puritans were known to shake or come under the influence of the Holy Spirit. It was said that they had enthusiasm! When Paul preached with the enthusiasm from the Holy Spirit, it moved the people who heard him. He said his preaching stirred in the minds of his hearers "most holy emotions and thus persuading them" (1 Cor. 2:4, AMP). Therefore, we can see the protocol of the Holy Spirit never changes.

Follow church history from the book of Acts through the present-day Spirit filled church. You can find many accounts of Christians experiencing what they called "holy laughter." The outpouring of the Holy Spirit which took place in the early 1900's in Azusa Street was also witnessed around the world. From the charismatic revival in the sixties and seventies to this generation— there are the same demonstrations of the Holy Spirit. Though looked down on by some religious hierarchy, it is true that the wisdom of God will confound the wise (1 Cor. 1:27). The effect of the anointed preaching of the Gospel continues to stir in the minds of those who hear, the most holy emotions. It is joy unspeakable and full of glory. The result is that our faith does not stand in the wisdom of men, but in the power of God.

BE CONTINUALLY FILLED
BECAUSE YOU LEAK

The Holy Spirit prompts us to rejoice so we can be filled with Him. Why do you have to be continually filled with the Holy Spirit? Because you leak! Paul said in Ephesians 5:18, "And be not drunk with wine, wherein is excess; but be filled with the Spirit." In the Greek, it literally means to "be-being filled." We require a continuous refilling.

Everyone acts different when they are filled with the Holy Spirit. Some people are full of joy at church and as soon as they leave, they return to their whining and complaining. They leaked!

God, through the power of the Holy Spirit, desires to change our minds so we're not thinking little. One man told me, "If I believed like that I think I'd lose my mind!" I said, "Go ahead, lose your mind and get the mind of Christ!"

> *As you yield to the Spirit of the Lord He has power over your intellect, over your heart, and over your voice. The Holy Spirit has power to unveil Christ and to project the vision of Christ upon the canvas of your mind, and then use your tongue to glorify and magnify Him in a way that you could never do apart from the Spirit's power.* [3]
> - *Smith Wigglesworth*

Some people have the Holy Ghost tied up and gagged in the basement! You can barely hear Him saying, "Let me out." You say, "No, if I let you out, You'll have me witnessing to somebody. The last time I let You out, You had me getting happy and dancing. Then I gave more money in the offering than I had planned to give. I'm not going to let you out!"

Jesus said that the Holy Spirit has come to live in you forever. As you yield to Him, He will have power over your intellect, think through your mind and change your personality. You may say, "I don't know about that!" Think about this — you have the media, your grandma's opinion or things you picked up at college all trying to think through your mind. The Holy Spirit is the Spirit of Truth and He will speak truth to your mind from God's Word. When you respond to Him and act on that Word, there is power that will be released. "If you continue in my Word, then you are my disciples indeed; and you shall know the truth, and the truth shall make you free. If therefore the Son shall make you free, you shall be free indeed." (John 8:31 – 32, 36). That's when every need is met.

SHOW YOUR TEETH

You can be holy and happy! You can walk around and smile. You can show your teeth! I like to say, "The toothbrush was invented in Arkansas. If it were invented anywhere else, they'd call it a teethbrush!" (We tease people from the state of Arkansas about not having teeth). You can't get a sad Holy Ghost. No, He takes the things of Christ and the Good News and makes them real to us.

On the day of Pentecost, they all had fire on their heads. The Holy Spirit had come upon them. Now, you can't have fire on your head and act normal! The Holy Spirit will start a celebration in you over the victory Christ already won at Calvary, just like He did back then. Someone once said, "A fly never lands on a hot stove." Beelzebub is a name for the devil and means lord of the flies. So if you stay on fire, the devil won't land on you.

I like what Smith Wigglesworth said, "We are commanded by God to be filled with the Spirit, and in the measure that you fail of this you are that far short of the plan of God. We can apprehend Christ fully only as we are filled and overflowing with the Spirit of God. Our only safeguard from dropping back into our natural mind from which we can never get anything, is to be filled and yet filled again with the Spirit of God and to be taken on to new visions and revelations." [3] He also said, "It is a luxury to be filled with the Spirit, and at the same time it is a divine command." [3]

Jesus commanded the disciples before He ascended back to Heaven, to go to the upper room and be clothed with power from on high – to be filled with the Holy Spirit. You can't get a sad Holy Ghost, but when we are filled with Him, we are filled with righteousness, peace and joy unspeakable. You can't be any closer to Jesus than you are yielded to the Holy Spirit. So go ahead, obey God's command and make a habit of drinking the living water and be continuously filled with joy and the Holy Ghost!

And the disciples were continually filled [throughout
their souls] with joy and the Holy Spirit.
- *Acts 13:52 (AMP)*

The disciples had been preaching in Antioch and had a revival going. The revival even broke out among the Gentiles. Of course, the devil didn't like this and neither did the Jewish religious leaders. They stirred up such trouble that the disciples had to leave town. Before they left they shook off the dust of that city and went on their way full of joy and the Holy Ghost. What do you do when people are lying about you and persecuting you? Jesus said to rejoice and be exceedingly glad (Matt. 5:12).

Peter encouraged the persecuted church to not think it strange when they had a fiery trial, but to rejoice when you share Christ's suffering. He said, "when His glory shall be revealed, ye may be glad also with exceeding joy" (1 Peter 4:13).

The proper protocol before God and in the middle of trouble has never changed. It still brings supernatural results; it is joy unspeakable and its results are the glory of God.

[1] *Merriam Webster. (n.d.). Retrieved September 2011, from An Encylcopedia Britannica Company: www.merriam-webster.com.*

[2] *enthusiasm. (n.d.) The American Heritage Dictionary of the English Language, Forth Edition. (2003). Retrieved 2012 http://www.thefreedictionary.com/enthusiasm.*

[3] *Wigglesworth, S. (2001). Ever Increasing Faith. New Kensington, PA: Whitaker House.*

The Kingdom of God is...righteousness, and peace
and joy in the Holy Ghost. - Romans 14:17

And my message and my preaching were very plain.
Rather than using clever and persuasive speeches, I
relied only on the power of the Holy Spirit.

- 1 Corinthians 2:4 (NLT)

9

Demonstrations of Joy In the Holy Ghost

The disciples were filled with joy and the Holy Ghost.

- *Acts 13:52*

Everywhere the Apostle Paul went, he endeavored to function supernaturally as opposed to the way he had been trained up. He had been a very strict, religious man who even went so far as to persecute and help stone many Christians, including Stephen.

After being knocked to the ground by the glory of God on the road to Damascus, and after meeting Jesus there, the last thing he wanted was more religion. Those scales fell from his eyes when he was filled with the Holy Ghost.

He warned that if he was "beside himself" or "mad," it was Christ's fault (2 Cor. 5:13). Paul must have studied David's life and the Psalms, but when he was filled with the Holy Spirit, he experienced the reality, power and fire of the Holy Ghost joy. Look at what he wrote in 1 Corinthians 2:

> *And my speech and my preaching was not with enticing words of man's wisdom, but in demonstration of the Spirit and of power: That your faith should not stand in the wisdom of men, but in the power of God.*
>
> *- 1 Corinthians 2:4 – 5*

I like the way verse 4 reads in the *New Living Translation*, "And my message and my preaching were very plain. Rather than using clever and persuasive speeches, I relied only on the power of the Holy Spirit." Paul relied on the Holy Spirit – the Spirit Who takes what Christ has done for us and makes it real in us. He takes the Word out of rhetoric into reality.

DEMONSTRATIONS OF THE HOLY SPIRIT

Do we have any record of demonstrations of the power of the Holy Spirit upon people? The answer is yes!

You may say, "They don't act like that in my church." My answer is, "We're not in your church!" Or you may say, "Jesus didn't act like that." But everyone He touched did! He is still touching people today.

In the book of Acts, we see not only the gifts of the Holy Spirit working through anointed people, but we see the effects the power had on those who were touched by that fire. They are the same effects today. Let's look at some demonstrations of the Holy Spirit throughout the Bible and in the early church.

RUNNING

In 1 Kings 18, we read the account of the prophet Elijah praying earnestly for rain seven times. Seven times he bowed down praying, not stopping, until the servant came back to report a cloud the size of a man's hand. As soon as Elijah heard that, he instructed the servant to tell Ahab to hitch up his chariot quickly because rain was coming. Look at what happened next.

> *In a little while, the heavens were black with wind-swept clouds, and there was a great rain. And Ahab went to Jezreel. The hand of the Lord was on*

> *Elijah. He girded up his loins and ran before Ahab*
> *to the entrance of Jezreel [nearly twenty miles].*
> - *1 Kings 18:45 - 46 (AMP)*

Elijah out-ran the chariot when he heard and believed the servant's report. I like verse 46 in the *Message Bible* because of the picture it gives: "And God strengthened Elijah mightily. Pulling up his robe and tying it around his waist, Elijah ran in front of Ahab's chariot until they reached Jezreel."

Throughout the Bible, rain signifies the blessing of God or the power of the Holy Spirit being poured out. In places where the Word comes forth and people receive it, believe it and respond, you will often see demonstrations of running. My mother was a runner! She was delivered from depression through the Word and the anointing it released in her life. Every yoke of fear in her mind disappeared; her body was completely healed because of that anointing.

> *And it shall come to pass in that day, that his*
> *burden shall be taken away from off thy shoulder,*
> *and his yoke from off thy neck, and the yoke shall*
> *be destroyed because of the anointing.*
> - *Isaiah 10:27*

Later, any time my mother sensed that anointing that set her free, she would take off running. When she ran, many others were set free by the same anointing and joy would fill the place.

Another outstanding miracle took place in a woman who responded to the anointing as I preached in one of our services. She began to run and just continued to run. As she ran, the power of God was working. We didn't know it at the time, but she had been diagnosed with six incurable diseases. She was healed of every one of them that night as she responded to the anointing and ran!

LEAPING

Leaping is a demonstration of joy that is a response to the Word and to the anointing. As seen in John the Baptist, even a baby can respond to the anointing.

> *And it came to pass, that, when Elisabeth heard the salutation of Mary, the babe leaped in her womb; and Elisabeth was filled with the Holy Ghost.*
> *- Luke 1:41*

Leaping was also the response of the crippled man who was healed at the gate called Beautiful. As I mentioned earlier in the book, when Peter commanded him to rise and walk in the Name of Jesus, "...he leaping up stood, and walked, and entered with them into the temple, walking, and leaping, and praising God" (Acts 3:8). So we see that leaping is a proper response to the word of the Lord.

SINGING

In the New Testament, both Elisabeth and Mary responded to God's Word to them by singing prophetically. Ephesians 5 tells us to be filled with the Spirit by singing.

> *And be not drunk with wine, wherein is excess; but be filled with the Spirit; Speaking to yourselves in psalms and hymns and spiritual songs, singing and making melody in your heart to the Lord.*
> *- Ephesians 5:18 - 19*

Paul taught and practiced this in Acts 16 as he prayed and sang songs so loudly that all the prisoners heard. Heaven came down and glory shook the entire jail!

Moses, Deborah, David and many others sang prophetically after great victories were won. Jesus sang hymns before his crucifixion, and in Hebrews 2:12 (AMP), "For He says, I will declare Your [the Father's] name to My brethren; in the midst of the [worshiping] congregation I will sing hymns of praise to You."

The Lord thy God in the midst of thee is mighty; he will save, he will rejoice over thee with joy; he will rest in his love, he will joy over thee with singing.
- *Zephaniah 3:17*

If you think about it, even the longest book in the Bible is a song book! Singing is simply a result of the Spirit of Liberty setting you free. The Jews in Psalm 126 were set free and they declared, "Then was our mouth filled with laughter, and our tongue with singing: then said they among the heathen, The Lord hath done great things for them" (vs. 2).

GREAT JOY

Wherever the Word is preached with the anointing there should be a response of joy. David said he rejoiced over the Word as one who found a great spoil (Ps. 119:162). If you found a quarter, a dollar or even a twenty, you would be happy. But if you received a very large inheritance or gift, you'd be shouting, jumping, and waving your arms around. You'd be full of smiles and laughter! That's the proper response when God speaks to you through His Word! Let's look at some examples in scripture.

The wise men had this kind of joy at Jesus' birth. "When they saw the star, they were thrilled with ecstatic joy" Matt. 2:10 (AMP). The women had it at Jesus' resurrection: "So they went out quickly from the tomb with fear and great joy, and ran to bring His disciples word," Matthew 28:8 (NKJV).

The early Church was filled with joy and the Holy Ghost. "And there was great joy in that city," Acts 8:8. "And the disciples were filled with joy, and with the Holy Ghost," Acts 13:52. Paul and Barnabas saw this joy wherever the Word went forth. "And being brought on their way by the church, they passed through Phenice and Samaria, declaring the conversion of the Gentiles: and they caused great joy unto all the brethren," Acts 15:3.

The Holy Spirit confirms the preaching of the Word with signs following (Mark 16:20). One of those signs is great joy!

DRUNK IN THE SPIRIT

After being filled with the Holy Spirit on the Day of Pentecost, the believers were accused of being drunk by the people who saw them. Peter didn't deny it, but told them that it was not as they supposed (Acts 2:15). The 120 that were in the upper room were not filled with wine, but with the Holy Spirit. They were prophesying and magnifying God in unknown languages.

Ephesians 5:18 tells us not to be drunk with wine where there is excess, but to be continually filled with the Holy Spirit. One of the outward demonstrations of the inward filling is acting drunk or under the influence of the Holy Spirit. How do many people act when they are under the influence of alcohol? They are happy, singing, bold, outspoken, and full of joy!

LAUGHTER

There are two kinds of laughter. One is for joy and celebration. It does good like a medicine and brings health and refreshing.

> *Then was our mouth filled with laughter....*
> *- Psalm 126:2*

> *And Sarah said, God hath made me to laugh, so that all that hear will laugh with me.*
> *- Genesis 21:6*

The other kind of laughter is a mocking laugh to be used toward God's enemies or your enemies.

He that sitteth in the heavens shall laugh: the Lord shall have them in derision.

- Psalm 2:4

The Lord shall laugh at him: for he seeth that his day is coming.

- Psalm 37:13

At destruction and famine thou shalt laugh....

- Job 5:22

What has happened when a Spirit-filled Christian begins to laugh an anointed laugh? They may be "taking their medication" or they may be "drawing water from the wells of salvation" and drinking from the Holy Ghost. There has been a breakthrough in their understanding. They see that they are seated with Jesus far above any situation and that the devil is under their feet. They see every problem from a new perspective of victory in Christ. Their laughter is a demonstration of Satan's defeat. It shows that the battle is won and victory is theirs!

GENEROSITY

An immediate effect and demonstration of the Holy Spirit is great generosity. Acts 2:46 says, "They worshiped together at the Temple each day, met in homes for the Lord's Supper, and shared their meals with great joy and generosity" (NLT). "And so it turned out that not a person among them was needy. Those who owned fields or houses sold them and brought the price of the sale...," Acts 4:34 (MSG).

DANCING

Dancing is seen throughout the Bible—even today —as a demonstration of joy or victory. The response to something good happening is the same in every culture and among the young and old. Is it in the Bible? One classic example of dancing in the Bible is found in Exodus. When Miriam, Moses sister, picked up her tambourine and sang and danced after the Egyptian army was destroyed in the Red Sea (Exodus 15:20).

Another dancer in the Bible was David. In 2 Samuel 6, the Ark of the Covenant was coming into Jerusalem. The Bible says that when the Ark came into the city, King David danced before the Lord with all of his might (vs.

14). <u>*Moffatt's*</u> translation says, "David whirled before the Eternal with all his might in the dance." <u>*The New English Bible*</u> says, "David, wearing a linen ephod, danced without restraint before the Lord." <u>*Goodspeed's*</u> translation says he was: "whirling in a dance with all his might." David's dancing expressed his joy in the presence of God. It was proper protocol for bringing the glory of God back into the nation.

THE FATHER LIKES IT WHEN YOU DANCE

I remember one time as I was leaving my place of prayer, the Holy Ghost said, "You're not going to dance? The Father likes it when you dance." So I just started dancing around the best I could, praising God. Suddenly, the Holy Ghost came on me. I thought, "He does like that! I believe I'll do that again!" I found out that one of the greatest things this did was crucify my flesh, because my flesh did not want to act like that!

David humbled himself by dancing as the Ark came into Jerusalem. Like him, we can bring the glory into our families, churches, and nations as we humble ourselves to dance before the Lord in the spirit.

Dad Hagin said, "There is a blessing that comes on me when I dance in the spirit that I can get no other way."

A minister watched a girl dancing with joy and asked God to give him a dance like that. He said the Holy Spirit told him, "A dance is not something I give you, but is something you give Me."

SHOUTING

David said, I offer in His tabernacle sacrifices of joy (Ps. 27:6). Other translations render this, "sacrifices of shouting." What does that look like? Can you imagine David getting in the presence of God and forgetting everything else? There was no other way to express his joy but with loud shouts of praise!

> *And now shall my head be lifted up above my enemies round about me; in His tent I will offer sacrifices and shouting of joy; I will sing, yes, I will sing praises to the Lord.*
> *- Psalm 27:6 (AMP)*

When the Holy Spirit is moving, there will be a demonstration of joy. Yield to Him, and watch God turn your life around!

We rejoice in His mercy

We rejoice in His grace

We rejoice in His presence

We rejoice before His face

10

The Power of Joy and Praise

I will bless the Lord at all times: his praise shall
continually be in my mouth.
- Psalm 34:1

When I was a teenager, I went to Tanzania to stay with missionaries Ralph and Shirley Hagemier for the summer. I remember going out into the bush to preach in churches and the way they praised still stands out to me today. The African Christians lifted their voices to praise with all their heart and strength. I did the American style of praising for about 30 seconds and thought I was finished. But those believers wouldn't stop until the pastor finally went to the pulpit and began to ring a bell. He told me they had a problem. They did not know when to stop praising God. I told him we had a similar problem in America, but it was the opposite—we had to play all kinds of music to even get them started!

I was really put to shame by a lady who caught my attention by her loud shouts of joy and praise. She was handicapped because she had no legs, but she was "out-praising" everyone else in the church! She understood Psalm 103:1, "Bless the Lord, O my soul: and all that is within me, bless his holy name."

Praise is vocal. It can be seen and heard by others. We see a great example of this in Acts 16. Paul and Silas were imprisoned, their hands and feet bound in stocks, but the authorities forgot to tape their mouths shut! I like to say that as long as you have your voice, there's no prison that can hold you.

At midnight, as Paul and Silas prayed and sang praises unto God—loud enough for the other prisoners to hear them—something began to happen.

And suddenly there was a great earthquake, so that
the foundations of the prison were shaken: and

immediately all the doors were opened, and every

one's bands were loosed.

- *Acts 16:26*

Paul and Silas did what many Old Testament prophets and minstrels did in times of trouble. They believed what God had spoken, sang His praises (Ps. 34:1, Ps. 105:43, and 2 Chron. 20:21-22) then watched as He showed up and turned their situation around!

God will do the same for you. Psalm 50:23 says, "Whoso offereth praise glorifieth me: and to him that ordereth his conversation aright will I shew the salvation of God." The Hebrew word for "praise" here is *towdah* which means "an extension of the hand, or (usually) adoration; specifically, a choir of worshippers:—confession, (sacrifice of) praise, thanks (-giving, offering)." [1] When you praise and thank God, it is a sacrifice that results in a breakthrough in your situation.

YOUR VOICE IS YOUR ADDRESS

I like to say that your voice is your address in the realm of the spirit! The Holy Spirit always fell wherever the Word was preached or somebody started praising. Some folks substitute applause for opening their mouth to praise

God, but salvation comes to the ones who lift their voices. Whenever we find ourselves in a position where our help has to come from God alone, that's when we can offer a sacrifice of praise and thanksgiving to Him and expect Him to show us His salvation. His salvation is His deliverance, safety, provision, preservation, and soundness. We must confess, or acknowledge, what He has declared in His Word to be true in our present circumstances. And we must do it continually. Hebrews 13:15 says, "By him therefore let us offer the sacrifice of praise to God continually, that is, the fruit of our lips giving thanks to his name." *The Amplified Bible* translates this verse: "Through Him, therefore, let us constantly and at all times offer up to God a sacrifice of praise, which is the fruit of lips that thankfully acknowledge and confess and glorify His name."

God is watching over His Word to perform it, but we must open our mouths and praise—and not just occasionally. We must be like David who proclaimed, "His praise shall continually be in my mouth," Ps. 34:1. He was a man who knew how to tap into the anointing by singing praises to His God.

As believers we should follow David's example in praise. However, ours is a greater advantage and privilege under the new covenant. Let's tap into that anointing like David did. As the *Message Bible* says in Hebrews 13:15, "Let's take our place outside with Jesus, no longer pouring out the sacrificial blood of animals but pouring out sacrificial praises from our lips to God in Jesus' name."

THE PRAISE CURE

I love the story Dr. Lilian B. Yeomens tells in her book, <u>Healing From Heaven.</u> She tells the story of a missionary to China who had ministered fearlessly to a sister missionary with smallpox.

> *Then a very bad case of confluent smallpox (that was what it looked like to the doctors) came out on her. Not knowing what to do, this missionary went before the Lord. He told her to sing and and praise Him for His faithfulness to His Word.*
>
> *And that's exactly what she did. Though she was isolated to prevent the smallpox from spreading and told by her doctor to lie quietly, this woman sang and sang and praised and praised. She said that if she didn't praise God, the very stones would cry out.*
>
> *The doctor said he feared for her life—that the case was serious and awful complications threatened. But this woman missionary just sang and sang and*

praised and praised.

He said she was evidently delirious, but that he had so little help he couldn't restrain her. So she just sang and sang and praised and praised. She was told that if by any chance she recovered, she would be disfigured for life. She sang and praised louder than she ever had before.

Finally, they asked this missionary, "Why do you praise so much?" She answered, "Because I have so many pox on me. God shows me I must praise Him for each one separately." And she kept right at it.

The Lord had shown her a vision of two baskets— one containing her praise, which was half full, and the other containing her testing, which was full. He told her that the praise basket must be filled so that it would outbalance the other. And so she kept at it. Her songs and shouts were so Spirit-filled they were contagious. The Christian nurses couldn't resist joining in and they kept the place ringing! At last, the Lord showed her that the praise basket was full and overflowing. She saw it sink and the testing basket rise in the air. In only a moment it seemed, the smallpox and all its symptoms vanished, leaving not even the trace of a single scar.

Yes, the praise cure works every time for everyone and it is not at all unpleasant! Rather, it is delightful to those who partake of it and its cost has been met for us by another, by a man—Jesus Christ. Because Jesus took the stripes on his back, this cure is available—at this very moment—to each of us. [2]

Are you ready to begin the praise cure? The last clause of 1 Peter 1:8 tells us exactly how to begin: "...believing, ye rejoice with joy unspeakable and full of glory."

ONLY BELIEVE

Just believe what the Word says Jesus has done for you. Think about it, talk about it, sing about it, shout about it, and the praise cure has begun. Remember, do this continually. Don't just take this cure once a year, but take it every day. Make it a part of your lifestyle, and watch as God goes to work on your behalf!

When Trina was diagnosed with an inoperable brain tumor, I spoke to that tumor and told it to die and leave her head in Jesus' Name. Then we surrounded ourselves with praise and singing until the day she was wheeled into the operating room for a biopsy to determine the nature of the tumor. All the way into surgery, she laughed until she went under the anesthesia. After a few hours, the surgeon appeared with a puzzled but happy face. He reported the operation revealed that the tumor—the very same one that showed up on every test—had completely disappeared! When you rejoice, something is happening back at the ranch!

PRAISE MOVES HEAVEN

God has tied Himself irrevocably to human cooperation in the work of redemption. He has made man's faith a determining factor in the execution of Divine purposes. [3]

- Lilian B. Yeomens

Have you ever felt like not one or two, but three problems were surrounding you? That's the time to move up into God's methods of deliverance! I like what Dr. Yeomens said about receiving a miracle: "God is not only going to do what He says; He is going to do it exactly as He says." [3] There is a divine protocol!

We find a classic example of how to cooperate with God in the execution of divine purposes in 2 Chronicles 20. King Jehoshaphat found himself up against three armies set on his destruction. Following divine protocol, he gathered the nation together to fast and seek the Lord. As they stood to magnify God and recount past victories, the Spirit of God came upon Jahaziel to prophesy and give Heaven's battle plan. Then they all bowed down to worship and stood together in praise. The next morning something amazing happened. Let's take a closer look at what happened.

And they rose early in the morning, and went forth into the wilderness of Tekoa: and as they went forth, Jehoshaphat stood and said, Hear me, O Judah, and ye inhabitants of Jerusalem; Believe in the Lord your God, so shall ye be established; believe his prophets, so shall ye prosper. And when he had consulted with the people, he appointed singers unto the Lord, and that should praise the beauty of holiness, as they went out before the army, and to say, Praise the Lord; for his mercy endureth for ever. And when they began to sing and to praise, the Lord set ambushments against the children of Ammon, Moab, and mount Seir, which were come against Judah; and they were smitten.

- 2 Chronicles 20:20 - 22

As Jehoshaphat and his people took the position of praise—as they followed divine protocol—God fought the battle for them. It took them three days to gather the spoil of that battle!

No matter what battle you're facing today, the divine strategy is to send praise ahead of you. We see this again and again in the Word. Judges 1:1–2 says, "Now after the death of Joshua it came to pass, that the children of Israel asked the Lord, saying, Who shall go up for us against the Canaanites first, to fight against them? And the Lord said, Judah shall go up: behold, I have delivered the land into his hand." Judah means "praise." Here again, God's strategy is to send the praisers in first. Send the praisers first and the battle shall be won!

OPEN YOUR MOUTH AND SHUT THE DEVIL UP

T.D. Jakes says, "If you don't rejoice, the devil will think he's winning!" In Matthew 21:16, as Jesus entered Jerusalem in His triumphal march, He quoted Psalm 8:2, "Out of the mouth of babes and sucklings hast thou ordained strength because of thine enemies, that thou mightest still the enemy and the avenger." He used the word strength in place of the word praise when he quoted this verse. Why? He was facing the biggest battle ever fought for the salvation of all humanity. What preceded His great victory over death, hell, and the grave? Joyful praise! When you praise and magnify God, it brings His strength into your situation. Then it shuts the mouth of the devil and all the voices of doubt and fear.

Romans 4:12 tells us to walk in the steps of the faith of Abraham. What are those steps? Abraham always believed and then praised. When you believe God's promises, you have the faith of God. When you praise God, He reaches into your future and changes everything.

That's exactly what Abraham did before he became the father of Isaac. "He staggered not at the promise of God through unbelief; but was strong in faith, giving glory to God; And being fully persuaded that, what he had promised, he was able also to perform," Rom. 4:20–21. Your praise will cause you to be fully persuaded! No doubt! It is DONE! The victory is WON! Praise is detergent that washes doubt out.

Take your position of faith today and praise God for His mercy. Let your mouth sacrifice praises. See His salvation, rejoice with joy unspeakable and full of glory, and receive what you're believing for! "O magnify the Lord with me, and let us exalt His name together," Ps. 34:3. "Bless the Lord, O my soul, and all that is within me, bless His holy Name," Psalm 103:1. Don't let anyone praise for you or out praise you. Your praise will bring salvation to your address.

[1] *James Strong, The New Strong's Exhaustive Concordance of the Bible (Nashville: Thomas Nelson Publishers, 1984) H8426.*

[2] *Lilian B. Yeomans, M. (12th Printing 2003). Healing from Heaven. Springfield, MO: Gospel Publishing House.*

[3] *Lilian B. Yeomans, M. (2003). Healing Treasury: Four Classic Books on Healing, Complete in One Volume. Tulsa, OK: Harrison House.*

Shout to testify of your faith in God's promise and

thankfulness for His glorious mercy.

Shout to encourage yourselves and your brethren and

to strike terror into your enemies.

- John Wesley

For those tough stains, you've got to shout them out!

- Mark Hankins

Don't doubt - just shout! God will work it all out!

- David Shearin

11

Shout For Joy

And now shall my head be lifted up above my enemies round about me; in His tent I will offer sacrifices and shouting of joy; I will sing, yes, I will sing praises to the Lord.

- Psalm 27:6 (AMP)

I remember hearing my mother shout as she prayed in faith until she knew she had the answer. Whatever the situation, it changed as she began to shout! Many times she would quote Psalm 27:1-6 just to encourage herself. There is something in a shout of joy that releases the energy of God and propels a believer out of a place of defeat into complete victory!

We see examples in the Bible of victories that were won as God's people lifted up a great shout. At the battle of Jericho in Joshua 6, the children of Israel lifted up their voices and the walls of the city came down. In Judges 7, we see Gideon leading his army to triumph with a shout. There are also joyous shouts that connect with angelic hosts and usher in the glory of Heaven, such as on the night of Jesus' birth. These are occasions when Heaven and earth meet together to celebrate a victory won or bring the power of God on the scene.

Psalm 47:5 says that God has gone up with a shout. 1 Thessalonians 4:16 tells us that Jesus shall descend from Heaven with a shout. What is in this shout? This shout releases God's power called joy.

> *Let them shout for joy, and be glad, that favour my*
> *righteous cause: yea, let them say continually, Let*
> *the LORD be magnified, which hath pleasure in*
> *the prosperity of his servant.*
> - *Psalm 35:27*

The Hebrew word for this joy in Psalm 35:27 is *ranan* and means "to creak (or emit a stridulous sound), i.e. to shout (usually for joy):--aloud for joy, cry out, be joyful, (greatly, make to) rejoice, (cause to) shout (for joy), (cause to) sing (aloud, for joy, out), triumph."[1] A joyful shout is directly connected to prosperity and blessing from God! The same word *ranan* is used in Psalm 32:11 says, "Be glad in the LORD, and rejoice, ye righteous: and shout for joy, all ye that are upright in heart." It is released in response to God's deliverance, protection, and mercy. It is a joyful response to God's saving power (Is. 12:6). It is a universal sound, understood in any language, especially in the Church. Let us shout for JOY and be GLAD!

RELEASE YOUR AUTHORITY

Psalm 149:6-7 states that believers are to "Let the high praises of God be in their mouth, and a two-edged sword in their hand; To execute vengeance upon the heathen, and punishments upon the people." The shout of praise releases the believer's authority over the enemy!

The enemies we are up against are not people, but principalities, powers, rulers of the darkness of this world and spiritual wickedness in heavenly places (Eph. 6:12). If you could only see demonic activity in the spirit realm, you would run to church and learn how to use your authority as a blood-washed believer! Jesus has already spoiled those principalities and powers, making a display of their defeat (Col. 2:15). 2 Corinthians 2:14 says that God always causes us to triumph in Christ.

DON'T DOUBT - JUST SHOUT AND GOD WILL WORK IT ALL OUT

Psalm 47:1 tells us to shout to God with the voice of triumph. The Hebrew word in this verse for shout is ruwa' and its meaning is: "to mar (especially by breaking); figuratively, to split the ears (with sound), i.e. shout (for alarm or joy): —blow an alarm, cry (alarm, aloud, out), destroy, make a joyful noise, smart, shout (for joy), sound an alarm, triumph." [1] This is a shout that connects the believer to the triumph of Christ. This is a shout that executes our God-given authority over anything that may have come to steal, kill, or destroy—a shout that releases the high praises of God and strikes fear in every enemy of God! So when you are up against something that seems too difficult to overcome, or a sin that has stained your soul, there is power in the blood to remove it. When you realize this fact, you can open your mouth and shout praise to God! There is a time to pray and then there is a time to praise God for the victory.

FOR THOSE TOUGH STAINS, YOU'VE GOT TO SHOUT THEM OUT!

Be glad in the Lord, and rejoice, ye righteous: and shout for joy, all ye that are upright in heart.

- *Psalm 32:11*

There is a laundry product formulated to remove tough stains called "Shout." In the commercial advertising this wonder working product, that would make any housewife smile, they say, "For those tough stains, you've got to shout them out!"

You can shout out the tough stains in your life. God specializes in removing even the most difficult stains and bringing great deliverance when people look to Him in prayer and acknowledge His power with a shout of praise! Let's look at a story from the Bible where God's power was released as His people shouted.

> *And when Judah looked back, behold, the battle was before and behind: and they cried unto the Lord, and the priests sounded with the trumpets. Then the men of Judah gave a shout: and as the men of Judah shouted, it came to pass, that God*

> *smote Jeroboam and all Israel before Abijah and*
> *Judah. And the children of Israel fled before Judah:*
> *and God delivered them into their hand.*
>
> *- 2 Chronicles 13:14 - 16*

What did the "praisers" do in this instance? First, the priests sounded the trumpet. Then, all the men of Judah shouted with an ear-splitting sound and they gained the victory!

As believers, we are priests who should lift our voices in authority and signal to the Church to give a shout! Our "trumpet" is a shout! Send up your praise, shout first and God's power will be released. Remember, your part is to look to God, believe and cooperate with His purposes by releasing your authority, and to give a shout that moves Heaven and strikes terror in the enemy.

When Balak prophesied to the people of God, he could only bless them, saying "He hath not beheld iniquity in Jacob, neither hath he seen perverseness in Israel: the Lord his God is with him, and the shout of a king is among them," Num. 23:21. As the Church lifts its voice in a shout, Jesus, our King, inhabits our praise. His authority is released through our shouts of joy!

SHOUT TO RELEASE HEAVEN'S ARMIES

Do you want to see demons flee, sickness healed, and the battle won? Shout! Do you want to pray in faith and see mountains move? Shout!

> *I come across some people who would be giants in the power of God, but they have no shout of faith. I find people everywhere who fail, even when they are praying, simply because they are just breathing sentences without uttering speech; and you cannot get the victory that way. You must learn to take the victory and shout in the face of the devil, "It is done!" There is no man who can doubt if he learns to shout. Things will be different and tremendous things will happen.* [2]
>
> - *Smith Wigglesworth*

When you shout, you are trusting that God's favor and blessing is surrounding you like a shield. Can't you see that happening as the Holy Spirit makes this real to the Church today? Look at what Psalm 5 says:

> *But let all those that put their trust in thee rejoice: let them ever shout for joy, because thou defendest*

> *them: let them also that love thy name be joyful in*
> *thee. For thou, Lord, wilt bless the righteous; with*
> *favour wilt thou compass him as with a shield.*
>
> - Psalm 5:11 - 12

Your shouts of praise will surround you with a shield of favor and protection. During the tribal war in Zaire, our friend, Ralph Hagemier had a large missions compound that included houses, a church, a Bible School, a school for children and several other buildings. The rebel soldiers attacked them, killing some of their staff and students. They ransacked the buildings and stole a large amount of property. Most everyone had fled for their lives, but the Hagemier family was hiding, holding on to their remaining possessions.

One morning, Ralph had had enough! The Holy Spirit stirred him up with a holy anger and he decided to go after his stuff! His wife, Shirley, begged him not to go, but he was determined. He picked up his Bible and headed on foot over the hill towards the encampment of rebels. As he mounted the top of the hill, the anointing came on him and he lifted his hands straight up with his Bible held high, then gave a piercing shout!

Down in the camp, the soldiers heard him, looked at him and took off running in terror! Ralph went on into the camp and found all of his possessions. He got it all back! Later, he found out that as he stood on the hill top shouting, the rebels saw gigantic warrior angels with big weapons coming with him!

GOD'S HEAVENLY CAMPAIGNS

Throughout the Bible, God is called the Lord of hosts. I think the Lord and His hosts, which are angelic armies, showed up that day on the hills of the Congo. Strong's Concordance gives this meaning for the word "hosts", (tsbadah in Hebrew), which are angels who fight for the people of God and bring deliverance to people when they pray, praise, and shout for joy! This word means "a mass of persons (or figuratively, things), especially reg. organized for war (an army); by implication, a campaign, literally or figuratively (specifically, hardship, worship): - appointed time, army, battle, company, host, service, soldiers, waiting upon, warfare." [3]

Your Holy Ghost inspired shout is a heavenly campaign against your enemies and God's enemies. It releases the angels who work in coordination with God's plan, set times, and seasons. These angels helped to announce Christ's birth, attended Him in the garden, and will be present at His return. I like 1 Thessalonians 4:16 in *The New English Bible.*

> *For the Lord shall come down from heaven with a*
> *shout of command, with the voice of the archangel,*
> *and with the trumpet of God, and the dead in*
> *Christ shall rise first. Then we who are alive, who*
> *are left, will be suddenly caught up with them to*
> *meet the Lord in the air. And we will always be*
> *with the Lord.*
>
> - *1 Thessalonians 4:16 (NEB)*

Jesus will soon gather the Church to Himself with a shout! That means every time the devil hears believers shout, he thinks Jesus is coming back with all the hosts from Heaven! Revelation 19:1, 3, 6, and 7 in *The Amplified Bible* refer to shouting going on around the throne in praise to God. When we all get to Heaven, there is going to be some mighty shouting.

Take God's exceeding great promises as your own. Stand boldly upon His Word and begin to exercise the authority of His Name, His Word and Jesus' blood! Open your mouth when the Holy Spirit moves upon you to possess what belongs to you! Like David, you can pursue, overtake, and recover all that belongs to you. I like to quote

Abraham Lincoln, "The fight of today is not all together for today but for a bright future." Shout with the voice of triumph! Jesus has conquered and Satan is defeated! The enemy is under your feet!

John Wesley said, "Shout to testify of your faith in God's promise and thankfulness for His glorious mercy. Shout to encourage yourselves and your brethren and to strike terror into your enemies."

[1] James Strong, *The New Strong's Exhaustive Concordance of the Bible* (Nashville: Thomas Nelson Publishers, 1984) H7321.

[2] Wigglesworth, S. (2001). *Ever Increasing Faith*. New Kensington, PA: Whitaker House.

[3] James Strong, *The New Strong's Exhaustive Concordance of the Bible* (Nashville: Thomas Nelson Publishers, 1984) H6635.

Sing yourselves

into His presence.

- Psalm 100:2 (MSG)

12

Sing For Joy

Arise, and go down to the potter's house, and there I will cause thee to hear my words. Then I went down to the potter's house, and, behold, he wrought a work on the wheels. And the vessel that he made of clay was marred in the hand of the potter: so he made it again another vessel, as seemed good to the potter to make it.

- Jeremiah 18:2 - 4

I once visited a shop where pottery was made and they demonstrated the entire process. I saw the wheel and the kiln (an oven) where the pottery was fired to harden it. The potter told us that after the vessels were shaped they were placed in this kiln until they were done. He said they were finished when there was a high-pitched sound that came from the vessels. He called it "singing."

I began to think about our lives and some of the fiery trials we go through. Remember what 1 Peter 1:7 - 9 says:

> *That the trial of your faith, being much more precious than of gold that perisheth, though it be tried with fire, might be found unto praise and honour and glory at the appearing of Jesus Christ: whom having not seen, you love; in whom, though now ye see him not, yet believing, ye rejoice with joy unspeakable and full of glory: Receiving the end of your faith even the salvation of your souls.*
>
> *- 1 Peter 1:7 - 9*

According to the Word, we are going to experience "trials" of our faith. James 1:2-4 says, "My brethren, count it all joy when ye fall into divers temptations; Knowing this, that the trying of your faith worketh patience. But let patience have her perfect work, that ye may be perfect and entire, wanting nothing."

When we go through fiery trials, we are like that

pottery in the kiln. Our faith is tried by the fire. However, instead of us falling apart, the process of what God has begun in our life is completed. Instead of whining and crying, there is a song. When our Potter (God) hears a high-pitched sound, or singing, coming out of our vessels, He will bring us out perfect and we will receive the result of our faith! Isaiah 41:10 in *The Amplified* version says God will "strengthen and harden you to difficulties." He will make us vessels to be used by Him.

It is when joy and songs of praise are heard right in the middle of the fire that there is a release. Just think about Shadrach, Meshach, and Abed-nego in the fiery furnace (Daniel 3). They determined in their hearts not to bend their knees to any other god and when the heat was turned up, they remained steadfast in their faith. That's what Peter was talking about in 1 Peter 1:7, "That the trial of your faith, being much more precious than of gold that perisheth, though it be tried with fire, might be found unto praise and honour and glory at the appearing of Jesus Christ."

Because these men honored God when their faith was tried by fire, they stood the test and the Lord Jesus Christ stood with them. He was the fourth man who appeared in the fire! Shadrach, Meshach, and Abed-nego came out smelling sweet, without even a hair on their heads singed. God worked this situation not only for their good, but used it to turn the king and the entire nation around to serve and honor Him instead of idolatry!

HEAVEN'S HYPERBARIC CHAMBER

In the presence of the Lord there is fullness of joy, so it is the atmosphere of Heaven. It is Heaven's hyperbaric chamber! In the natural, if a person is suffering from a wound that needs the healing process to be accelerated, such as a diabetic would have, the doctor may prescribe some time to be spent in the hyperbaric chamber where there is a high oxygen level. As the patient receives treatment, he takes what is called a "dive" and must have assistance in walking because he is under the influence of the treatment. It has an effect similar to being intoxicated.

Likewise, when someone needs healing or a broken heart mended, the anointing of joy restores them to wholeness. It is Heaven's medicine! Proverbs 17:22 says, "A merry heart doeth good like a medicine: but a broken spirit drieth the bones." Let the atmosphere of Heaven pervade your life with healing as you "take your medicine."

LISTEN! JESUS IS SINGING!

Jesus, our High Priest Who ever lives to intercede for His dear children, sings over us in times of great trial. He is the sweet singer of Heaven who taught David how to sing his way to victory, time after time. When you sing, if you listen, you can hear Him! Hebrews 2:12, referring to Jesus, says this: "For He says, I will declare Your [the Father's] name to My brethren; in the midst of the [worshiping] congregation I will sing hymns of praise to You" (AMP). Jesus is singing praise to God! Those are called "songs of deliverance" (Psalm 32:7).

No matter what you're facing today, you can be confident because the Lord is with you. Hebrews 13:6 (AMP) says, "So we take comfort and are encouraged and confidently and boldly say, The Lord is my Helper; I will not be seized with alarm [I will not fear or dread or be terrified]. What can man do to me?"

Jesus knows about fiery trials. His trial was the greatest in history as He faced Pilate, hateful mobs, soldiers and even separation from God. What did He do before He entered this difficult time? After the Last Supper and before going into the garden, He led his followers in a hymn of praise (Mark 14:26). I can imagine it comforting

Him as He went to Calvary. He heard that song ringing in His heart. Maybe He remembered Psalm 32:6-7:

> *...Surely when the great waters [of trial] overflow, they shall not reach [the spirit in] him. You are a hiding place for me; You, Lord, preserve me from trouble, You surround me with songs and shouts of deliverance. Selah [pause, and calmly think of that]!*
>
> *- Psalm 32:6 - 7 (AMP)*

I like the <u>*New Living Translation*</u> of verse 7: "For you are my hiding place; you protect me from trouble. You surround me with songs of victory." Songs of deliverance or songs of victory surround the believer whose heart is trusting God. When trials come, they are not greater than the grace of God. God Himself is a strong tower of refuge, and in the secret place of the Most High there is a holy insulation against all the fiery trials. That song of deliverance is a sound coming directly from Jesus to deliver you and preserve your life from destruction.

Songs of deliverance are what saved my father-in-law, Bill Behrman, as he lay in a coma in an Italian hospital with a condition known as septicemia (bacteria in the blood). Through prayer and medical attention his life was saved, but he was in critical condition.

His condition began to turn for the better when Trina, her sister (Patsy), and her mother began to sing hymns at the house and praise God for His intervention. The next day when they went to visit her dad, he was sitting up and looking strong. When they asked what happened, he told them how he began to sing hymns in the ICU by himself the night before. He sang so loudly the nurses came in and told him he had to quiet down. Hallelujah! There's no distance in the spirit as believers turn on their expectation and lift their voices to God to praise Him!

That's exactly what Paul and Silas experienced when they were imprisoned – their feet shackled (Acts 16:23-26). In the darkness of night, they lifted their voices, singing hymns to God – and Jesus could have sang with them. The very moment Jesus began to sing, an earthquake took place that broke every shackle and opened every prison door. Listen, you can hear Him singing. Sing along. Sing yourself into His Presence (Psalm 100:2, MSG).

SPRING UP, O WELL

What can you do in those times when you feel dry or depressed? God had specific instruction for the children of Israel in Numbers 21.

> *That is the well whereof the Lord spake unto*
> *Moses, Gather the people together, and I will give*
> *them water. Then Israel sang this song, Spring up,*
> *O well; sing ye unto it:*
> *- Numbers 21:16 - 17*

God's instruction to His people was to gather together. There is power in unity and corporate gathering. The believers in Acts 4 gathered together as they were being persecuted for preaching Christ. When they did, they were filled with the Holy Spirit, boldness and joy. Here in Numbers, God promised that He would give the people water. They gathered together as the Lord had told them and began to sing to the well, "Spring up, O well!"

When we begin to sing together, God responds by sending refreshing water from the River of Life. Jesus referred to this River in John 7:37–38. He stood up and cried to the people to come to him and drink, telling them that from their innermost being would flow rivers of living water, or the Holy Spirit. Any time you sing and drink from these waters there will also be joy!

JOY COMES IN THE MORNING

Psalm 30:5 says, "...Weeping may endure for a night, but joy comes in the morning." There is a time to cry. Jesus wept deeply with Mary and Martha at the death of his friend Lazarus. He wept, but He had come on that day to bring life. Before He left, He turned their sadness into joy!

When you encounter loss and trial, the power of the Holy Spirit comes to bring you through to the other side. You are not left to your own strength, but He comes bringing salvation. Isaiah 12:2 says, "Behold, God is my salvation; I will trust, and not be afraid: for the Lord Jehovah is my strength and my song; he also is become my salvation." What does this salvation include? It includes deliverance, healing, safety, soundness, and preservation.

Think about Peter when he was walking to Jesus on the water. The moment he took his eyes off Jesus to look at the waves around him, he began to sink. He screamed, "Jesus, save me!" Instantly, the strong hand of the Lord reached down, grasped Peter, and pulled him up again. They walked back to the boat together (Matt. 14:28-32). That is salvation! The songs you sing in the night—the midnight hour of your life—will bring this salvation to you.

Go ahead and weep and cry. Play country songs and

get all your friends together and mourn, but when morning comes, put away your tears, cast your cares on the Lord, and decide to count it all joy. Sing and dance and forget what lies behind! Get ready to press toward what lies ahead! Joy comes in the morning!

Joy came for the king who threw Daniel in the lion's den. Instead of being eaten by ferocious lions, Daniel trusted in his God. The mouths of the lions were shut and he was delivered out of that den in the morning (Dan. 6).

Just as salvation came to Daniel, it also came to the 400 distressed, discontented and in debt men who David, I believe, taught to rejoice before God with singing, shouting and joy. They became his mighty men (1 Samuel 22:2; 2 Samuel 23:8-23).

During his many beatings and multiple shipwrecks, the Apostle Paul also learned to rejoice. In Philippians 4:4, he said, "Rejoice in the Lord always. And again I say, rejoice."

Even Jesus, our great example, was anointed with the oil of joy (Hebrews 1:9)! For the joy that was set before Him, He endured the cross and gained the victor's crown (Hebrews 12:2).

In times of trouble, you need to look to God. He is your Salvation—your Healer, Deliverer, and Provider. He is everything you need! Be a doer of the Word and come out on top—a vessel of honor with songs of joy! That joy is heavenly, triumphant joy and carries that glory of God! Get ready—you've got joy now and you are drawing salvation up.

SONGS OF REDEMPTION FROM THIS GENERATION

When I was a teenager, I had a friend who taught me to play the guitar and sing to God. I had the best times in my bedroom with the door shut, singing simple songs based on the Word that I was meditating on. I sure didn't sound professional and the dog may have howled at my singing, but I was singing to God. The Holy Ghost would come and we'd have a time! I may have started out depressed but I'd end up so happy just like David's mighty men.

There is something powerful about the revelation of redemption that releases a song to every generation.

And they sung a new song, saying, Thou art worthy to take the book, and to open the seals thereof: for thou wast slain, and hast redeemed us to God by thy blood out of every kindred, and tongue, and people, and nation.

- Revelation 5:9

Patsy Cameneti said, "When a generation comes to a revelation of redemption, they sing about it and add another verse to the Song of Redemption. In Heaven, you'll hear all the songs in all languages." Get ready to hear the old songs and the new songs that will be sung by the young generation. They'll sing out their revelation of all God has done to rescue, restore, and to revive. It will cause a mighty revolution that brings hope to this generation. Go ahead, let the singing begin.

Joy Unspeakable

I have found His grace is all complete,
He supplieth ev'ry need;
While I sit and learn at Jesus' feet,
I am free, yes, free indeed.

It is joy unspeakable and full of glory,
Full of glory, full of glory,
It is joy unspeakable and full of glory,
Oh, the half has never yet been told.

I have found the pleasure I once craved,
It is joy and peace within;
What a wondrous blessing! I am saved
From the awful gulf of sin.

I have found that hope so bright and clear,
Living in the realm of grace;
Oh, the Savior's presence is so near,
I can see His smiling face.

I have found the joy no tongue can tell,
How its waves of glory roll!
It is like a great o'erflowing well,
Springing up within my soul. [1]

13

The Secret Power of Joy

One night as I had prayed in my hotel room before a service, I heard the voice of the Holy Spirit reminding me to "make room" for Him. He reminded me of the words of an old preacher who encouraged me before I got up to preach and said, "Be bold with the gift of God!" I thought about the time in prayer when the Holy Spirit said to me, "You're going to give happy altar calls." That was the exact opposite from the crying, sad ones I had heard in church when I attended some services! The awareness of the Holy Spirit was more real to me than anything. He had come to help and I needed Him in order to minister to the people that night.

The church was full of people, some who came, not knowing what to expect. As I got up, the Holy Spirit gave a message of encouragement and joy. This is part of what He said:

> *Remember not the former things. Arise, for the glory of the Lord is risen upon you and the goodness of God shall be yours. I will turn your captivity, saith the Lord, and fill your mouth with laughter. Things that you have dreamed, things that you have believed for and you have desired for many years, you'll see now. There will be great progress towards those things and you'll laugh and say, 'Look what the Lord has done!' You will praise the Lord with a loud voice, declaring His faithfulness unto you; for not only will you go forward, but you will lead many others and they'll go forward too!*

That must have been exactly what they needed, because the place erupted with shouts of praise and expressions of joy! It sounded like a football game after the touchdown and by the end of the service, you could see we definitely had won the victory! There were shouts, songs, dances and happy faces everywhere. Later, some came forward to receive Christ and some gave testimonies about miracles that had happened in that joyful atmosphere. It was exactly as the prophecy said!

There's nothing I enjoy more than to see the words of Jesus fulfilled whenever the Good News is preached! As you have read this book, I pray you will have experienced the power of these words, the mission statement of Jesus Christ:

> *The Spirit of the Lord [is] upon Me, because He has anointed Me [the Anointed One, the Messiah] to preach the good news (the Gospel) to the poor; He has sent Me to announce release to the captives and recovery of sight to the blind, to send forth as delivered those who are oppressed [who are downtrodden, bruised, crushed, and broken down by calamity], To proclaim the acceptable year of the Lord [the day when salvation and the free favors of God profusely abound].*
>
> *- Luke 4:18 - 19 (AMP)*

---

[1] *Warren, B. E. (1900). Joy Unspeakable. (B. E. Warren, Performer)*

Wherefore seeing we also are compassed about with so great a cloud of witnesses, let us lay aside every weight, and the sin which doth so easily beset us, and let us run with patience the race that is set before us, Looking unto Jesus the author and finisher of our faith; who for the joy that was set before him endured the cross, despising the shame, and is set down at the right hand of the throne of God. For consider him that endured such contradiction of sinners against himself, lest ye be wearied and faint in your minds.

- Hebrews 12:1 - 3

14

Finish Strong!

When I was in junior high, I joined the track team at my school. I'll never forget the first 880 race I ran. Halfway through it I got tired and decided I was finished, so I got off the track, trotted across the field, and stood by the coach. He was watching for all the runners to come across the finish line and couldn't find me, so he hollered, "Where's Hankins?" I spoke up beside him, "Right here, Coach." Boy, was he ever mad at me! I guess the first lesson I learned in track was not to quit or try to take a shortcut, but to stay on course and finish my race—even if I was tired.

I have friends who run marathons and other long

races that require endurance. I have noticed that the physical and mental training process they undergo can be compared to the Christian race. One runner, Zale Tabakman, said this: "The skills required for success and the skills required for running a successful marathon are one and the same. Successful runners focus on a goal, are patient and realize everything takes time. We plan our training, we make sure we maintain our motivation and we gather people around us to help us."[1] Hebrews 12:2 in *The Amplified* says, "Looking away [from all that will distract] to Jesus, Who is the Leader and the Source of our faith [giving the first incentive for our belief] and is also its Finisher [bringing it to maturity and perfection]. He, for the joy [of obtaining the prize] that was set before Him, endured the cross, despising and ignoring the shame, and is now seated at the right hand of the throne of God."

FOCUS ON THE GOAL

Both Paul and Peter talk about the goal, the prize or the hope and inheritance. This goal kept them going when things got very hard. It's like runners in a race. They don't look down, but set their eyes on short goals, always remembering the final prize. In the same way, Peter encouraged the church not to forget the goal—the end of their faith. They were being persecuted and some were even killed, but this was no time to quit!

> *Blessed be the God and Father of our Lord Jesus*
> *Christ, which according to his abundant mercy*
> *hath begotten us again unto a lively hope by the*
> *resurrection of Jesus Christ from the dead, To*
> *an inheritance incorruptible, and undefiled, and*
> *that fadeth not away, reserved in heaven for you.*
> *Wherein ye greatly rejoice, though now for a season,*
> *if need be, ye are in heaviness through manifold*
> *temptations: That the trial of your faith, being*
> *much more precious than of gold that perisheth,*
> *though it be tried with fire, might be found unto*
> *praise and honour and glory at the appearing of*
> *Jesus Christ: Whom having not seen, ye love; in*
> *whom, though now ye see him not, yet believing,*
> *ye rejoice with joy unspeakable and full of glory:*
> *Receiving the end of your faith, even the salvation*
> *of your souls.*
> *- 1 Peter 1:3 - 4, 6 - 9*

When you think things look impossible and you're going through a great trial of your faith, keep on believing, speaking, and rejoicing! Even though you can't see Jesus, love Him and believe Him so much that you can't help but be full of joy unspeakable and full of glory. When you do that, you are receiving what you believe! You are headed to the finish line!

CHEERING FROM THE GRANDSTANDS

There is no purpose for a race without a goal. For the believer, that goal is receiving all you have believed God for and the ultimate prize of winning Christ. Hebrews 12:1-3 is a classic picture of the race we are in. We see the witnesses in the grandstands cheering us on and Jesus, the focus of our eyes. He is our example of how to focus on the prize so that we don't quit. He was looking at the joy before Him with every step toward Calvary.

Wherefore seeing we also are compassed about with so great a cloud of witnesses, let us lay aside every weight, and the sin which doth so easily beset us, and let us run with patience the race that is set before us, Looking unto Jesus the author and finisher of our faith; who for the joy that was set before him endured the cross, despising the shame, and is set down at the right hand of the throne of God. For consider him that endured such contradiction of sinners against himself, lest ye be wearied and faint in your minds.

- Hebrews 12:1 - 3

Just think of Him Who endured from sinners such grievous opposition and bitter hostility against Himself [reckon up and consider it all in comparison with your trials], so that you may not grow weary or exhausted, losing heart and relaxing and fainting in your minds.

- Hebrews 12:3 (AMP)

Jesus was seeing you and me. He was seeing the Father saying, "Well done!" He was practicing what He told His disciples in John 16:33, "...in the world you shall have tribulation; but be of good cheer: I have overcome the world." I'm so glad Jesus endured and didn't quit!

Jesus' course took Him through the dark valley of death and seemed like a place of defeat. However with joy as His strength, he has become our great example of how to finish your course with joy.

Therefore we do not lose heart. Even though our outward man is perishing, yet the inward man is

being renewed day by day. For our light affliction,
which is but for a moment, is working for us a far
more exceeding and eternal weight of glory, while
we do not look at the things which are seen, but at
the things which are not seen. For the things which
are seen are temporary, but the things which are not
seen are eternal.

- 2 Corinthians 4:16 - 18 (NKJV)

Paul wasn't looking at the trouble around him, because he had seen a vision of Jesus. That vision became his focus so he wouldn't run his race in vain. He kept his focus with the help of joy!

OIL FOR ENGINES WITH HIGH MILEAGE

I shall be anointed with fresh oil.
- Psalm 92:10

I walked into a store to look for some special oil for one of my cars and I noticed that there was a certain oil with special ingredients formulated for engines with a high mileage of 75,000 miles or more. If oil companies can make special oil for engines with high mileage, I'm sure God has a special oil for believers with high mileage! According to Isaiah 61:3, the anointing is the oil of joy and is so powerful that it heals the broken-hearted, sets captives free, and opens blind eyes.

Without proper oil changes, an engine will overheat, make a lot of racket, and eventually shut down. The anointing is the oil of joy and just as engines require an oil change to work right, we need a fresh anointing of the Holy Ghost.

I once had a young minister on my staff who took his car to the shop because it wouldn't run anymore. They checked the oil and asked when he had last put oil in it. He responded, "Oh, are you supposed to do that?" After realizing his engine was destroyed, he learned the truth that "ignorance is expensive!"

Many Christians put off getting refilled with the oil of joy and the Holy Ghost because they are ignorant about it, are too busy or don't think it's necessary. Don't be ignorant, but stay full of the Holy Spirit. It is necessary. But like my dad used to say when my mother would rejoice and run around the church, "It's not necessary unless it's necessary!"

Paul said, Rejoice in the Lord always; and again I say rejoice (Phil. 4:4). Maybe you've once been full of the oil of joy and the Holy Ghost, but now you've got high mileage, and you're clunking along, not getting anywhere! You need to stop, get refilled with the Holy Ghost and REJOICE!

THE OIL OF JOY

...Thou anointest my head with oil....
- *Psalm 23:5*

It shall come to pass in that day that his burden will be taken away from your shoulder, and his yoke from your neck, and the yoke will be destroyed because of the anointing oil.
- *Isaiah 10:27 (NKJV)*

You love justice and hate evil. Therefore, O God, your God has anointed you, pouring out the oil of joy on you more than on anyone else.
- *Hebrews 1:9 (NLT)*

There's no mountain too big for you to move, no assignment too difficult to finish, and no city too great for you to possess if you stay full of the oil of joy! Joshua and Caleb—the only spies to bring back a good report from the Promised Land—could have sat in their rocking chairs, put up their feet, and talked about the good old days, at the end of their lives. Instead, they must have been staying in the presence of God, remembering what Moses told them about not being afraid and about meditating on God's Word. They must have started rejoicing over the promises of God. They stayed busy raising up the next generation to be strong, courageous and full of faith (Numbers 13-14; Joshua 1). As they did, they were anointed with fresh oil. They were headed to their destination and the walls of Jericho had to come down!

In Bible times, when a runner prepared for a race in that arid climate, he would anoint his body with oil to protect it from excessive perspiration. When mixed with perfume, the oil imparted a delightfully refreshing and invigorating sensation. That is what happens spiritually as our Shepherd Jesus, anoints our heads with oil. When you are anointed with fresh oil of the Holy Spirit, you receive supernatural ability, endurance and strength. There is a refreshing in the joy of the Lord that will enable you to run strong and finish your particular race with joy! Isaiah 40:31 says "But they that wait upon the Lord shall renew their strength; they shall mount up with wings as eagles; they shall run, and not be weary; and they shall walk, and not faint." Receive the reward for your faith and enter into the joy of the Lord!

RUN TO WIN

You've all been to the stadium and seen the athlete's race. Everyone runs; one wins. Run to win. All good athletes train hard. They do it for a gold medal that tarnishes and fades. You're after one that's gold eternally.

- 1 Corinthians 9:24, 25 (MSG)

This race of faith begins and ends with Jesus. He is the Author and Finisher. He is the goal and the prize. He is the joy we are focused on! Even when we can't see Him with our eyes, we believe and love Him so we don't get distracted, looking to the right or left. Instead, we should do like one marathon runner told me they did to keep focused. They kept their watch in view so they could keep a steady pace and listened to happy music so they wouldn't get bored and quit. Most of all, they kept their mind on the goal—the finish line.

Peter knew the agony of quitting on Jesus and learned his lesson. There was no stopping Peter when he repented and believed. He was filled with the Holy Spirit and started running his race! Peter wrote these words which are the theme of his life and of this book:

Whom having not seen, ye love; in whom, though now ye see him not, yet believing, ye rejoice with joy unspeakable and full of glory: Receiving the end of your faith, even the salvation of your souls.

- 1 Peter 1:8 - 9

Just as the runner said earlier in this chapter, "Successful runners focus on a goal, are patient and realize everything takes time. We plan our training, we make sure we maintain our motivation and gather people around us to help." In the same way, that's how we finish our course with joy! Jesus Christ, the Anointed One, was anointed with the oil of joy (Heb. 1:9). Throughout his life, He was trained in the Scriptures and learned obedience through the things He suffered. He stayed motivated by focusing on the reward, the joy of winning the prize. He fellowshipped with the Father, taught His disciples to pray and was empowered by the anointing of joy.

James said to count it all joy when you have all kinds of trouble. Patience and endurance will give you staying power and bring you to the goal. Remember the devil is impatient, but if you get full of joy, start dancing and shouting, he will soon give up. Your rejoicing is faith in action! We're not going to quit halfway. The joy and cheer of the Holy Spirit is our strength.

F. F. Bosworth was a man greatly used by God in the area of healing in the early 1900's. He saw countless people saved and many healed of all kinds of sicknesses and conditions. He also wrote the classic book, <u>*Christ The Healer.*</u>

When he was in his eighties, Bosworth announced one day that he would be going to Heaven soon. He wasn't sick, but he was ready to go. On his death bed, he told his family goodbye and then began to see into the glory realm. He began to call out the names of acquaintances who had gone to Heaven before him. His wife recognized the names and realized he was getting ready to step across into Heaven. Sure enough, he soon sat up in the bed, lifted his hands, and shouted triumphantly, "I have fought a good fight, I have finished my course, I have kept the faith: Henceforth, there is laid up for me a crown of righteousness. Hallelujah!" Then Brother Bosworth fell back on the bed, absent from his body, but present with the Lord. [2]

With his last breath, Bosworth quoted Paul in 2 Timothy 4:7-8. In that same chapter, you can read how many other men had forsaken Paul, but he said the Lord stood by him, strengthening him and delivering him from all evil work. He finished strong and did all that Jesus told him he would do. Likewise, Brother Bosworth had been misunderstood and forsaken by some in his later years, but he finished strong. He finished his course like Paul. He was not disappointed or bitter, but full of joy!

I THINK MYSELF HAPPY

When I get to Heaven, I want to check out the video of Paul standing before King Agrippa! (I think there will be videos of all the great Bible stories.) I would have loved to have been in the palace with the king and his sister Bernice, as they walked in with great pomp. _The Message Bible_ says it this way.

> *The next day everybody who was anybody in Caesarea found his way to the Great Hall, along with the top military brass. Agrippa and Bernice made a flourishing grand entrance and took their places. Festus then ordered Paul brought in.*
> - *Acts 25:23 (MSG)*

Here was Paul, a short man with chains on his hands and feet, knots on his head from being stoned, and a few teeth missing. King Agrippa and Bernice had just come from the mall, dressed in their finest. I'm sure Bernice had just gotten her fingernails done, and all of the people were in high style. However, none of them were happy except for this one man in chains. He was on course, and he was happy. In one translation, Paul says, "I'm congratulating myself!" There is no chain that can bind up the spirit of a person who is full of joy and the Holy Ghost. Just look at what Paul told the king.

> *I think myself happy, king Agrippa, because I shall answer for myself this day before thee touching all the things whereof I am accused of the Jews: Whereupon, O king Agrippa, I was not disobedient unto the heavenly vision.*
> *- Acts 26:2, 19*

When Paul testified before King Agrippa, he realized he was in the exact place Jesus Christ had told he would be years before on the road to Damascus. Here he was, giving witness of Jesus to King Agrippa. He was demonstrating something he wrote about in Philippians 4:12–13:

> *I know how to be abased and live humbly in straitened circumstances, and I know also how to enjoy plenty and live in abundance. I have learned in any and all circumstances the secret of facing every situation, whether well-fed or going hungry, having a sufficiency and enough to spare or going*

without and being in want. I have strength for all things in Christ Who empowers me [I am ready for anything and equal to anything through Him Who infuses inner strength into me; I am self-sufficient in Christ's sufficiency].

- Philippians 4:12 - 13 (AMP)

I have learned in any and all circumstances the secret of facing every situation—I can do all this through Him who gives me strength. I like to say, "Paul had been snake bit, beat in the head, and left for dead, yet he could still stand up and say, 'I am more than a conqueror!'"

Even when he was forced to spend the end of his life in chains, Paul still wrote the book of Philippians – a short letter that mentioned joy and rejoicing 16 times. The joy of the Lord is our strength to finish strong.

RECEIVE THE REWARD WITH JOY

Whom having not seen, ye love; in whom, though now ye see him not, yet believing, ye rejoice with joy unspeakable and full of glory: Receiving the end of your faith, even the salvation of your souls.

- 1 Peter 1:8 - 9

Go ahead and receive the reward for your faith and enter into the joy of the Lord! You can then say, "I have fought a good fight, I have finished my course, I have kept the faith: Henceforth there is laid up for me a crown of righteousness!" When my mother took her last breath, her family was around her bed singing hymns and encouraging her to go on to meet Jesus. As she drew her last breath, there was some shouting going on in that room because we knew this praising, shouting joyful mother had entered into the joy of the Lord forever! It was "worth it all" because she had finished her course with joy. She taught me the "Secret Power of Joy!" There is victory and eternal joy in this life and in the life to come!

She used to sing this song, "It Will Be Worth it All."

It will be worth it all
when we see Jesus!
Life's trials will seem so small
when we see Christ.
One glimpse of his dear face,
all sorrow will erase.
So, bravely run the race
till we see Christ. [3]

This song really puts everything into perspective. Our eyes are set on Jesus, the prize and He gives us joy for the journey. We will run to the finish, finish with joy, and FINISH STRONG!!

[1] *Tabakman, Z. (n.d.). Success Through Balance © Practical Actions For Success. Retrieved 2011, from www.zaletabakman.ca.*

[2] *Bosworth, F. (2001). Christ the Healer. Grand Rapids, MI: Revell.*

[3] *Rusthoi, E. K. (Composer). (1951). It Will Be Worth it All. [E. K. Rusthoi, Performer].*

Mark Hankins Ministries

P.O. BOX 12863 ALEXANDRIA, LA 71315
318.767.2001 • contact@markhankins.org
Visit us on the web: www.markhankins.org

Reference Page

Asher, D. (2009). *The Egyptian Strategy for the Yom Kippur War: An Analysis.* Jefferson, NC: McFarland.

Barclay, W. *New Testament Words. Louisville, KY: Westminister John Knox Press.*

Bosworth, F. (2001). *Christ the Healer. Grand Rapids, MI: Revell.*

Breyer, M. (2011, August 23). *Care2 Make a Difference.* Retrieved January 2012, from Care2: www.care2.com/greenliving/8-health-benefits-of-laughter.html

Dictionary, Noah Webster's 1828 American. (n.d.). Retrieved December 2011, from www.1828-dictionary.com

Dr. Dwenda Gjerdingen, M. M. (2012). *The Network A Called Community of Women.* Retrieved January 2012, from http://ag.org/wim/index.cfm

Hayford, J. (2002). In J. Hayford, *The Spirit Filled Life Bible* (p. 17). Nashville, TN: Thomas Nelson Publishers.

Lewis, C. (2002). *Letters to Malcolm. New York, NY: Harcourt, Inc.*

Lilian B. Yeomans, M. (12th Printing 2003). *Healing from Heaven. Springfield, MO: Gospel Publishing House.*

Lilian B. Yeomans, M. (2003). *Healing Treasury: Four Classic Books on Healing, Complete in One Volume. Tulsa, OK: Harrison House.*

Meares, Aaron, diligentsoul.wordpress.com

Merriam Webster. (n.d.). Retrieved September 2011, from An Encylcopedia Britannica Company: www.merriam-webster.com

Miles, C. A. (1912, March). *In The Garden*. (C. A. Miles, Performer)

Nelson, P. (29th Printing 2007). *Bible Doctrines*. Springfield, MO: Gospel Publishing House.

Richman, C. (1997). *The Holy Temple of Jerusalem*. Jerusalem, Israel: Carta.

Rusthoi, E. K. (Composer). (1951). *It Will Be Worth it All*. [E. K. Rusthoi, Performer]

Strong, James. *The New Strong's Exhaustive Concordance of the Bible* (Nashville: Thomas Nelson Publishers, 1984)

Sumrall, L. (1995). *Pioneers of Faith*. Maple City, MI: Sumrall Publishing.

Tabakman, Z. (n.d.). *Success Through Balance © Practical Actions For Success*. Retrieved 2011, from www.zaletabakman.ca

Warren, B. E. (1900). *Joy Unspeakable*. (B. E. Warren, Performer)

Wigglesworth, S. (2001). *Ever Increasing Faith*. New Kensington, PA: Whitaker House.

About the Authors

Mark and Trina Hankins travel nationally and internationally preaching the Word of God with the power of the Holy Spirit. Their message centers on the spirit of faith, who the believer is in Christ, and the work of the Holy Spirit.

After over forty years of pastoral and traveling ministry, Mark and Trina are now ministering full-time in campmeetings, leadership conferences, and church services around the world and across the United States. Their son, Aaron, and his wife Errin Cody, are now the pastors of Christian Worship Center in Alexandria, Louisiana. Their daughter, Alicia Moran, and her husband Caleb, pastor Metro Life Church in Lafayette, Louisiana. Mark and Trina have eight grandchildren.

Mark and Trina have written several books. For more information on Mark Hankins Ministries, log on to the website, www.markhankins.org.

Acknowledgments

Special Thanks to my wife, Trina.

My son, Aaron and his wife, Errin Cody; their daughters, Avery Jane and Macy Claire, their son, Jude Aaron.

My daughter, Alicia and her husband, Caleb; their sons, Jaiden Mark, Gavin Luke, Landon James, and Dylan Paul, their daughter Hadley Marie.

My parents, Pastor B.B. and Velma Hankins, who are now in Heaven with the Lord.

My wife's parents, Rev. William and Ginger Behrman.

Mark Hankins Ministries Publications

SPIRIT-FILLED SCRIPTURE STUDY GUIDE

A comprehensive study of scriptures in over 120 different translations on topics such as: Redemption, Faith, Finances, Prayer and many more.

THE BLOODLINE OF A CHAMPION - THE POWER OF THE BLOOD OF JESUS

The blood of Jesus is the liquid language of love that flows from the heart of God and gives us hope in all circumstances. In this book, you will clearly see what the blood has done FOR US but also what the blood has done IN US as believers.

TAKING YOUR PLACE IN CHRIST

Many Christians talk about what they are trying to be and what they are going to be. This book is about who you are NOW as believers in Christ.

PAUL'S SYSTEM OF TRUTH

Paul's System of Truth reveals man's redemption in Christ, the reality of what happened from the cross to the throne and how it is applied for victory in life through Jesus Christ.

THE SECRET POWER OF JOY

If you only knew what happens in the Spirit when you rejoice, you would rejoice everyday. Joy is one of the great secrets of faith. This book will show you the importance of the joy of the Lord in a believer's life.

11:23 – THE LANGUAGE OF FAITH

Never under-estimate the power of one voice. Over 100 inspirational, mountain-moving quotes to "stir up" the spirit of faith in you.

LET THE GOOD TIMES ROLL

This book focuses on the five key factors to heaven on earth: The Holy Spirit, Glory, Faith, Joy, and Redemption. The Holy Spirit is a genius. If you will listen to Him, He will make you look smart.

THE POWER OF IDENTIFICATION WITH CHRIST

Learn how God identified us with Christ in His death, burial, resurrection, and seating in Heaven. The same identical life, victory, joy, and blessings that are In Christ are now in you. This is the glory and the mystery of Christianity – the power of the believer's identification with Christ.

REVOLUTIONARY REVELATION

This book provides excellent insight on how the spirit of wisdom and revelation is mandatory for believers to access their call, inheritance, and authority in Christ.

FAITH OPENS THE DOOR TO THE SUPERNATURAL

In this book you will learn how believing and speaking open the door to the supernatural.

THE SPIRIT OF FAITH

The Spirit of Faith is necessary to do the will of God and fulfill your divine destiny. Believing AND speaking are necessary ingredients in the spirit of faith. If you ONLY knew what was on the other side of your mountain, you would move it!

DIVINE APPROVAL: UNDERSTANDING RIGHTEOUSNESS

One of the most misunderstood subjects in the Bible is righteousness. The Gospel of Christ is a revelation of the righteousness of God, and the center of the Gospel reveals the righteousness of God. Understanding you have GOD'S DIVINE APPROVAL on your life sets you free from the sense of rejection, inadequacy or inferiority.

GOD'S HEALING WORD by Trina Hankins

Trina's testimony and a practical guide to receiving healing through meditating on the Word of God. This guide includes: testimonies, practical teaching, Scriptures & confessions, and a CD with Scriptures & confessions (read by Mark Hankins).